Ecotourism:
The Potentials and Pitfalls

Volume 2—Country Case Studies

World Wildlife Fund is the leading private organization in the United States working wildwide to protect endangered wildlife and wildlands. It is the U.S. affiliate of the international WWF family, which includes 22 other national organizations and 4 associates.

Ecotourism:
The Potentials and Pitfalls

Volume 2—Country Case Studies

by Elizabeth Boo

WWF

World Wildlife Fund
Washington, D.C.

Ecotourism: The Potentials and Pitfalls
Volume 2—Country Case Studies

Cover design by Supon Design Group, Washington, D.C.
Printed by Wickersham Printing Company, Inc., Lancaster, Pennsylvania.
Second printing, August 1992.

Volume 1: $10.00	Shipping and handling charges are $2.00 for
Volume 2: $12.50	the first title, $1.00 for each additional title
Set: $22.50	(or $2.00 for a set).

Book orders and payment should be directed to WWF Publications, P.O. Box 4866, Hampden Post Office, Baltimore, Maryland 21211. Telephone: (410) 516-6951.

Library of Congress Cataloging-in-Publication Data
Boo, Elizabeth.
   Ecotourism: the potentials and pitfalls / by Elizabeth Boo.
     p. cm.
   Vol. 2 has also apecial title: Country case studies.
   Includes bibliographical references.
   ISBN 0-942635-14-0 (v. 1). — ISBN 0-942635-15-9 (v. 2).
   1. Tourist Trade—Environmental Aspects. I. World Wildlife Fund.
II. Title.
G155.A1B6 1990   89-70735
338.4'791—dc20   CIP

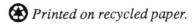 *Printed on recycled paper.*

Contents

Acknowledgments

Author
Elizabeth Boo

Principal Contributors
Katrina Brandon
Dennis Glick

Tourism Consultants
Susanne Frueh
Mystie McCormick
Don Hawkins
Jan Laarman

Field Researchers
Hector Ceballos-Lascurain
Antonio Torres
Yanina Rovinski
Marie-Jose Edwards
Victor Gonzales

Reviewers
Curtis Freese
Natalie Waugh
Jane Horine
John Wilson

Executive Summary Writer
Sarah Fitzgerald

Researchers
Lois Morrison
Alan Ragins
George Shillinger

Administrative Assistants
Catherine Monaghan
Carol Baker

Translators
Angela Mast
Isabel Ramos

Preparation of this study has been supported by a grant to World
Wildlife Fund by U.S. Agency for International Development.

CHAPTER 1

BELIZE

I. Status of Tourism Industry

A. History and Growth

The tourism industry is rapidly changing in Belize in terms of demand and supply. Not only is the number of tourists greatly expanding, but also, the government has recently started a campaign to improve tourism infrastructure and to develop the industry. Tourist arrivals increased by 55 percent between 1980 to 1987 from 63,735 to 99,266. The contribution of tourism to foreign exchange earnings grew from U.S. $41.0 million to an estimated $47.3 million in 1987 (Miller, 1988). Forecasts for the next three years estimate that tourist spending will increase approximately 7 percent annually (Tourism Report II).

According to 1986 World Tourism Organization (WTO) statistics, over 40 percent of visitors came from the United States that year, and almost 5 percent came from Canada. European visitors made up almost 20 percent of the visitors, with roughly half of these from England. (One reason for the high number from England is that Belize was formerly British Honduras until it became independent in 1981.) The remaining 35 percent of the visitors in 1986 is the combined figure for all other countries. (WTO, 1988).

WTO figures for seasonality patterns indicate that January through April is the high season, with monthly tourist arrivals in those five months comprising about 10 percent of annual arrivals. September through November is the low season, with average monthly arrivals at about 6 percent of the annual total.

Recent employment statistics for Belize indicate that in 1987 almost 9,000 people worked directly or indirectly in the tourism sector. Compared to the two previous years for which statistics exist, direct and indirect employment has been increasing at 6 to 8 percent per year. There have been increases in several service areas, such as dive boats. One operator recorded an increase of about 40 percent in tour boats between 1980 and 1987. (Tourism Report II).

Table 1.

TOURISM DIRECT AND INDIRECT EMPLOYMENT INCREASE

YEAR	DIRECT NO. OF EMPLOYEES ACCOMMODATION SECTOR	INDIRECT NO. OF EMPLOYEES OTHER SECTORS	TOTAL NO. OF EMPLOYEES
1985	2,590	5,180	7,770
1986	2,740	5,480	8,220
1987	2,980	5,960	8,940

Source: Tourism Report II, 1988

B. Major Tourism Attractions

Belize has a spectacular combination of natural and cultural resources. Natural resources include marine and coastal areas as well as wildlands in the interior. Cultural richness can be seen in the variety of native peoples that live in Belize as well as its many archeological sites.

The majority of Belize's environment is intact. Among its chief water resources is the second-largest barrier reef in the world (after the Great Barrier Reef in Australia). The reef runs more or less parallel to the entire length of the Belizean coastline for 115 kilometers (185 miles). Also, three of the four atolls found in the Atlantic Ocean are in the territorial waters of Belize. An atoll is a ring-shaped coral island surrounding a lagoon; the Belizean atolls are Lighthouse Reef, Turneffe Reef, and Glover's Reef. On Lighthouse Reef is Half Moon Caye Natural Monument, the oldest reserve in Belize.

Included in these waters is the famous "Blue Hole" explored by Jacques Cousteau during the 1970's. The "Blue Hole" is a mysterious underwater shaft more than 122 meters (400 ft) deep, featuring magnificent underwater stalactite formations. In addition, Belize has about 200 cayes off its shoreline. All of these water resources offer an abundant diversity of fish and coral. There are also many scenic sandy beaches along the southern shores.

Much of the tourism in Belize has developed around its marine ecosystems, and these resources continue to be the biggest attraction for tourists. The most visited marine area is San Pedro, Ambergris Caye, where scuba diving and snorkeling have

2

been popular activities for many years. Hol Chan Marine Reserve, a 12-square-kilometer (4.5-square-mile) area at the south end of Ambergris Caye, was recently established as a park and is receiving many divers.

Sport fishing is also very popular in the marine areas. The great abundance of habitat throughout the mangrove and reef system produces an ideal environment for the sport fisherman. Tarpon, grouper, snapper, permit, bonefish, barracuda, and other tropical species abound on the reef and in the flats. Billfish, guna, wahoo, mackerel, and other deep-sea fish thrive outside the reef in the deep waters.

In the interior, Belize has a diverse flora and fauna, with a large variety of bird and wildlife species from both the northern and southern hemispheres, many of which are rare or extinct in other parts of the earth. For example, the world's only jaguar sanctuary is in Belize. In addition, there are extensive jungles and pine forests.

Some of the most visited wildland areas include Mountain Pine Ridge, a 24,290-hectare (60,000-acre) reserve in the central and southern portion of Belize. The Cockscomb Jaguar Sanctuary is in the Maya Mountains of the Stann Creek District and protects prime jaguar habitat. The Crooked Tree Sanctuary, located 53.2 kilometers (33 miles) outside of Belize City, consists of a network of inland lagoons, swamps, and waterways; it is key to the protection of resident and migrant birds.

Another important wildlife attraction is the Belize Zoo, just outside of Belize City. Established in 1982, the zoo has a theme: "walk through Belize." Visitors walk down a forest path through four major habitat areas and observe the animals in their natural environments. The zoo has played a significant role in environmental education in Belize.

In terms of cultural resources, there are indigenous groups concentrated throughout Belize. These include the Mayas, occupying Toledo, the southernmost district of Belize. Both the Mopan and the Kekchi still live in their own communities. There is also the Garifuna community in Stann Creek District, which still maintains many African traditions.

Belize was an integral part of the Mayan world in the Classical period and was a major trading center for the area. More than 600 Mayan archeological sites have been excavated in Belize. Some of the most visited are Altun Ha, a major ceremonial center of the Mayan Classical period, located 30 miles north of Belize City. The jades from Altun Ha (Stone Water) are among the largest and most beautifully carved ever discovered. Xunantucich, which is west of Belize City and

Belmopan, near the Guatemalan border, is the most extensively and systematically excavated site in Belize.

The modern town of Corozal is built over the ancient Maya Center of Santa Rita. Archaeological investigations have shown Santa Rita to be in the ancient province of Chetumal, where a large part of the Post Classic civilization once thrived. Lamanai is one of Belize's largest ceremonial centers. In addition to its display of the more exotic features of the ancient Maya in art and architecture, Lamanai also has one of the longest continuous occupation spans, dating from 1500 B.C. to the 19th century. The largest ceremonial center, Caracol, sits on a low plateau in the Chiquibil Forest Reserve in primary rain forest jungle. Uxbenka is a site noted for its more than 20 stelae, at least seven of which are carved.

In terms of city attractions, Belize City receives the most visitors. Although deposed as the capital when it was almost destroyed by Hurricane Hattie in 1961, Belize City remains the heart of the country as its commercial and entertainment center.

C. Tourism Policy, Management, and Promotion

Until the recent advent of government support, tourism development in Belize was almost entirely self-propelled. Most tourism developed around San Pedro on Ambergris Caye, where considerable capital investments were made to attract the international scuba-diving community. Much of this tourism development was controlled by various factions of small entrepreneurs. These entrepreneurs include locals, foreigners, residents, and absentee owners, each following their own motives and business practices (BNTMP, 1988).

The administration previous to the present one listed tourism as its fourth priority for economic growth (New Belize, 1984) and it was not until the election of 1984 that the new government made tourism the second priority in its strategy for growth. Since this new recognition of tourism's importance, it is estimated that total direct revenue from tourism increased from U.S. $549,900 in 1985 to $762,300 in 1987 (see Table 2). Despite the increase in revenue, government tourist bureau employees claim that the hotel tax is to a large extent undercollected. It is estimated that the government could receive 50 percent more if all revenues were received. (Tourism Report, II).

4

Table 2.

DIRECT GOVERNMENT REVENUE FROM TOURISM (U.S.$)

YEAR	HOTEL TAX	LICENSES	PARK FEES	AIRPORT TAX	TOTAL
1985	117,500.00	1,400.00	2,000.00	429,000.00	549,900.00
1986	159,300.00	1,300.00	2,100.00	431,000.00	593,700.00
1987	206,700.00	1,400.00	2,200.00	552,000.00	762,300.00

Source: Tourism Report II, 1988

In 1988, the government issued its "Integrated Tourism Policy and Strategy Statement." This statement outlines the benefits and drawbacks of tourism development, the objectives of tourism development, and the players and methods to achieve these objectives. In terms of the economic and social benefits of tourism, the government notes that the gross, and in particular the net, foreign exchange receipts are very high in tourism compared to other sectors. It also recognizes that the tourism industry is labor-intensive and thus creates many jobs. The government estimates that each job directly related to tourism generates or supports two indirect jobs. It also states that government income from direct and indirect taxes may exceed 40 percent of revenues from stayover visitors.

The objectives of the government's tourism policy are to increase the number of stay-over visitors, maximize visitor expenditures, create a suitable investment climate including appropriate legislation to attract developers, provide capital for the expansion of tourism infrastructure and services, and to establish a tourism administration to coordinate tourism activities in the country.

Among potential drawbacks of tourism development, the government cites disadvantages to local investors who have difficulty competing with foreign investors. Also mentioned are foreign exchange leakages as well as over-reliance on the tourism sector at the cost of the growth of other subsistence sectors.

The government realizes that to develop the tourism industry, it must establish the means to generate reliable

5

statistics about tourism. To date there have been difficulties in determining critical information regarding tourism, such as precise figures for visitors, direct and indirect employment figures, and gross and net foreign exchange receipts and their contribution to government revenues.

In its strategy statement, the government identifies some specific projects it intends to undertake to develop tourism. Projects include the extension and improvement of the Philip Goldson International Airport in Belize City as well as the construction and improvement of airport facilities near San Ignacio and Placencia; development of nature and adventure trails and access roads to other natural areas; development of water, electricity, sewage, and telecommunications facilities; custom and immigration services at the country's air, sea, and road entry points; medical facilities in the major tourism areas, including at least one decompression chamber; and improvement of security measures throughout the country.

The government has also declared that it will grant numerous Import Duty Concessions to developers in the tourism sector, mostly in the accommodation sector. It will increase the percentage of import duty waiver from between 50 to 100 percent for improvements of Belizean-owned hotels and related services.

In terms of transportation, the government is also considering a three-year moratorium for transportation operators of import duty on specified types of transportation. The government also wants to expand the number of international airlines that offer service to Belize.

In laying out its tourism policy, the government gives special attention to the importance of natural resources in tourism development. The policy notes that Belize's natural areas are often referred to as a well-kept secret. However, the government points out, many of the country's scenic sites have to be prepared for tourism use and need to be better protected than they are at present. Thus, greater emphasis will be given to the Mayan ruins and caves; the Cockscomb and other forest areas that are still intact; the reefs, rivers, and lagoons; and the construction of an Anthropology-Natural History-Archeology Museum in Belmopan.

The government also identifies who will participate in tourism development. The Ministry of Tourism is the governmental office that will take the lead. In addition, the government plans to appoint an interministerial Tourism Development Committee of permanent secretaries from the Ministry of Tourism, the Ministry of Economic Development, the Ministry of Natural Resources, and the Ministry of Agriculture.

The government is trying to decentralize the mechanisms it uses to achieve its objectives. It has established the Belize National Tourism Council (BNTC), which comprises key government ministers and an equal number of individuals from the private sector of tourism. BNTC operates as an advisory body to the Ministry of Tourism, with its main emphasis on policy matters, and will soon be upgraded to a statutory board. The Belize Export Investment and Promotion Unit (BEIPU) is a private sector institution that has non-voting government representatives on its board. The BEIPU is involved with marketing and investment promotions in the tourism industry. Further, the government hopes to expand its marketing efforts through the establishment of the Belize Tourist Bureau (BTB).

The Belize Tourism Industry Association (BTIA) represents the private sector and works with the government on tourism development. BTIA has successfully revitalized connections among tour operators. The BTIA produces a monthly newsletter on tourism and brings together hoteliers, travel agencies, tour operators, and conservation groups. BTIA is investigating the possibility of offering off-season package deals for Belizeans so that they will be able to report from firsthand experience to tourists about Belize's tourism attractions.

The government statement highlights the need to integrate public and private sector efforts in tourism's growth. It also states the importance of diversification of the tourism product.

The main concentrations of tourist accommodations are found in Belize City (572 rooms), Ambergris Caye (278 rooms), and other cayes (198 rooms). In addition, some 160 rooms are located in the northern district, for a national total of 1,471 rooms. Current accommodation figures reflect a significant increase since the early 1980s, a change that tourism analysts attribute to increasing demand for nature tourism (Tourism Report II).

A local hotel manager claims that about 30 percent of his hotel guests visit Belize because of their interest in the flora and fauna of the country. All sites such as San Pedro, which is primarily visited by divers and fishermen, or Cha Creek Lodge in the mountains of western Belize, almost all the visitors come because of the natural environment.

Much of Belize's tourism infrastructure has been financed with foreign assistance or by foreign investors. The Belizean government is currently seeking more funds for tourism infrastructure. A recent agreement was made with the United Nations Development Programme (UNDP) and the World Tourism Organization (WTO) to formulate a model master development and zoning plan for Ambergris Caye. This would include plans for further infrastructure development, taking into account the need to determine saturation points and to decentralize around San

Pedro. It would also include plans for environmental protection. This model is considered the forerunner of 1) a general caye and reef development plan, and 2) district master development and zoning plans for Corozal, Cayo, and the southern mainland.

As part of its effort to promote the tourism industry, the government collaborated with the Caribbean Tourism Research and Development Center (CTRC) to conduct a survey in the winter of 1986. The Visitor Expenditure and Motivation Survey included over 2,300 persons. The purpose of the survey was to determine visitor profiles, purpose of visit, and expenditure patterns. (Miller, 1988)

Survey results indicated that about 72 percent of the tourists came to Belize for vacation, 19 percent for business purposes, and 9 percent for "other reasons," including visits to friends and relatives. Forty-one percent of the respondents reported that they had visited Belize previously, while 59 percent were on their first visit. The proportion of people on their first trip was higher among vacationers (65 percent) than among business travelers (42 percent).

On average, tourists spent 10.63 nights in Belize, with tourists from Canada and the United Kingdom staying longer than people from other countries. Three-quarters of the tourists stayed in paid accommodations (hotels, guest houses, motels).

About one-fifth of the tourists were traveling on an inclusive tour package, most of these from the United States. The tourists spent an average of U.S. $64.88 per person per day during their stay in Belize, or about U.S. $690 per person per visit based on the average length of stay of 10.63 nights. Of these expenditures, about half were for accommodations including room, food, and drinks purchased at the hotel. An additional 16 percent were spent on food and drinks outside the hotel, and the remainder went for other expenses.

The respondents were given a list of possible selected reasons for visiting Belize and asked to indicate which were "important" and which were "not important." The cayes/barrier reef was listed as "important" by the largest majority of people (37 percent), the climate was cited by 35 percent, the tropical setting by 35 percent and the "peace and quiet" by 31 percent. Surprisingly, the Mayan ruins were listed as "not important" by over 80 percent of the respondents (Visitor and Motivation Survey, 1986, as cited in Miller, 1988).

II. Status of Tourism to Protected Areas

A. Demand for Tourism to Protected Areas

There are several indicators of expanding demand for
tourism to protected areas in Belize. One is the increasing
numbers of tour operators who are focusing more of their tours
in natural areas. Secondly, there has been a tremendous growth
in small, often one or two person, tour services that have
emerged for the sole purpose of offering tours to parks and
reserves. These tour operators include: Adventure Belize Tours,
Aracari Outings, Caribbean Charter Services Unlimited, Explore
Belize Tours, Ltd., Personalized Services, Tiki Tours, and S&L
Guided Tours, all located in Belize. Operating outside Belize
are Belize American Trading Company, Belize Connection,
International Expeditions, International Zoological Expeditions
and Triton Tours, and Massachusetts Audubon.

Increased visitation has also been noted by hotel owners and
other travelers to Belize. In January, 1989, the manager of the
Pelican Beach Hotel in Dangriga said that this was the busiest
season ever in its history. The hotel had been filled to
capacity solidly for the previous six weeks. A recent visitor
claimed that he went to San Pedro and could not find a hotel
room.

To evaluate the demand for nature tourism, World Wildlife
Fund conducted surveys of tourists at the airport and at a
Belizean hotel. Tourists were asked to characterize the degree
to which natural protected areas influenced their travel plans
and activities. First, socio-demographic information was
collected from those surveyed. Then visitors were asked how
important protected areas were in their decision to visit the
country, how many protected areas they visited, and what kinds of
nature-oriented activities they participated in during the trip.

WWF Airport Survey Results

Socio-demographic Information

Average age:	40.5 years, with the youngest tourist being 18 years old and the oldest, 73 years old (N=80).
Average nights:	13.2 nights stayed. Shortest visit was 2 nights, longest was 99+ nights. (N=96).

9

Family members:	Thirty four (34 percent) of the 99 tourists interviewed were traveling with family members. Family groups averaged between two and three people (2.6). The minimum was with one other person (probably a spouse), and the largest group was one family of 10.
Expenditures:	The average for total trip-related expenditures was $1,490 (N=89), or an average expenditure of $157 per day. Of the 89 respondents to this question, 48 reported an average expenditure of $483 for international airfare. People who did not respond may have had airfare included in the price of a tour or were unsure of the cost.
Income:	The average family income range was between U.S. $30,000 and $40,000.
Gender:	58 percent men, 40 percent women, 2 percent no response.
Nationality:	The nationality distribution of the survey respondents (N=99) was as follows: 81.8 percent North American, 11.1 percent European, 2.0 percent Dominican Republic, 2.0 percent Australian, and 3.1 percent all other.

Protected Areas and Nature-oriented Tourism

When asked how important parks and protected areas were in their decision to visit, the majority indicated that it was important or very important to them and was an influence on their decision to travel to Belize. Responses given were as follows:

Main reason	8%
Important, influenced decision	36%
Somewhat important	29%
Not important	23%
No response	4%

10

This was the first trip to Belize for 72 percent of the visitors; for 28 percent it was a repeat visit. Most tourists had more than one reason to visit; the top five reasons given were:

Natural history	52%
Sightseeing	48%
Sun/beaches/recreation	47%
Archeology	44%
Cultural history	37%

Tourists to Belize engaged in a high proportion of recreational activities. Although 44 percent said that the parks and protected areas influenced their travel to Belize, many more tourists enjoyed nature-based activities. Over half of all tourists to Belize took a boat trip, watched birds, or went on a jungle excursion. Other nature activities had a high participation rate as well:

Boat trips	60%
Birdwatching	57%
Jungle excursions	56%
Wildlife observing	49%
Local cultures	34%
Hiking/trekking	30%
Mountaineering	22%
Botany	20%
Hunting/fishing	14%
Camping	5%

From the survey, 46 of the 99 visitors responded that what they liked most about Belize was the "friendliness of the people." Twenty-eight visitors listed the natural features and beauty of Belize. The most frequently listed dislike, indicated by 34 of the 99 visitors surveyed, was the "pollution, noise, and litter" in the country. Another commonly listed dislike recorded by visitors was the "road systems and the lack of signs" (23 visitors), and 16 visitors mentioned "crime."

B. The Supply of Protected Areas

1. Development and Management of Park System

The management of protected areas in Belize is unique in that there is currently no national park service, and the protected areas are managed by a nongovernmental organization. The Department of Forestry, the government agency in charge of the parks, has delegated management responsibilities for most areas to the Belize Audubon Society (BAS) until a park service is established, which is currently in process.

Before Belize became independent in 1981, the previous colonial government had created several reserves. In 1928, Half Moon Caye was established to protect the habitat of Belize's famous nesting colony of the Red-footed Booby. In 1977, the colonial government established seven tiny mangrove cayes to protect other sea-bird rookeries. In addition, 15 forest reserves, covering almost 20 percent of Belize, were created. The purpose of the reserves, however, was not wildlife conservation but timber exploitation.

The National Parks System Act, passed in 1981, is the legal foundation for establishing national parks, natural monuments, and wildlife reserves. Since this time, six additional parks have been declared.

2. Examples of protected areas:

Guanacaste Park

Guanacaste Park was established in 1973 and centers around a large guanacaste tree that supports an epiphyte colony of about 35 species of orchids, bromeliads, ferns, cacti, strangler figs and others. Given the park's small size of 21 hectares (52 acres), Guanacaste does not meet international size specifications for national parks.

Cockscomb Jaguar Sanctuary

The Cockscomb Jaguar Sanctuary is a 1,417-hectare (3,500-acre) site located within the Cockscomb Basin Forest Reserve protecting prime jaguar habitat and healthy populations of other wildlife species such as ocelot, margay, peccary, and deer. The sanctuary has a visitor center, cabins, an administrative building and many marked trails. At the entrance of the sanctuary in Maya Center, a gift shop was recently completed and is flourishing.

Bermudian Landing Howler Monkey Reserve

The Bermudian Landing Howler Monkey Reserve is a community-operated wildlife refuge that is primarily on private land. The reserve was established when it was discovered that a 25-kilometer (15.5-mile) stretch of riparian habitat near Belize City contained an extremely high population of howler monkeys (at least 800). Because most of this land is privately owned and some of it actually lies within a rural community, a mechanism was created whereby landowners voluntarily complied with a management plan drawn up by a biologist studying the monkeys. The community has developed a visitor center and is developing a bed and breakfast facility.

Hol Chan Marine Reserve

The Hol Chan Marine Reserve is a 5 square-kilometer (1.9 square-mile) transect that protects mangrove, reef, and deep water habitats. Established in 1987, it is a very popular area for fishing, diving, and snorkeling. The nearby town of San Pedro has an administrative office with an aquarium, marine exhibits, and interpretive materials.

Crooked Tree Wildlife Sanctuary

Crooked Tree Wildlife Sanctuary is located about 56 kilometers (35 miles) northwest of Belize City. It is 3.2 kilometers (2 miles) off the main highway and can be reached by a causeway that crosses an inland lagoon to the sanctuary. Established in 1984 for the protection of resident and migrant birds, the sanctuary consists of a network of inland lagoons, swamps, and waterways. During the dry season, thousands of birds congregate at Crooked Tree to take advantage of the food resources and to find a nesting spot on their spring migration north. Wildlife found within the sanctuary include the boat-billed heron, the chestnut-bellied heron, black-collared hawks, black howler monkeys, and morelet's crocodiles. There is a visitor center and marked trails.

Shipstern Wildlife Sanctuary

Shipstern Wildlife Sanctuary and Butterfly Farm is a privately owned protected area established in 1987 in the northeastern part of Belize. It encompasses 77 square-kilometers

(29.7 square-miles) of tropical forest, savanna, mangrove, and lagoon coastline. A major activity at the reserve is the breeding of butterflies. The concept behind the breeding program is to eventually export the pupae of several species of butterflies to England. The funds generated from the sale of these butterflies will be used for conservation of the reserve.

III. Impacts of Tourism to Protected Areas

A. Economic Activities Related to Nature Tourism

The economic impacts of tourism to protected areas can be seen in the number and growth of tour operators who focus on natural areas. Belize Travel Haus in Ambergris Caye has traditionally offered cultural history tours and is now starting to offer birdwatching and manatee-watching tours. Mountain Equestrian Trails is offering horseback riding excursions to the "wilds of the Mountain Pine Ridge Forest Reserve." S&L Guided Tours offers several nature tours including half-day, full-day and overnight excursions. Ricardo's is a small enterprise offering two- and three-day trips to an island along the barrier reef. Visitors stay in small guest cabins built over the water.

Economic activity can also be seen at individual protected area sites. For example, at Cockscomb Jaguar Preserve, no entrance fee is charged, but a small fee is charged to stay overnight in the rustic cabins. There are currently no eating facilities on site, so all food is brought into the preserve. The bigger economic impact is seen in the local community of Maya Center. The women have recently formed a cooperative gift shop to sell handicrafts to tourists. Since June they have sold U.S. $3,500 in handicrafts. Also, increasing numbers of guides from the village are being trained as tourist guides.

Economic impacts of tourism can also be seen at the Crooked Tree Wildlife Sanctuary. Nearby residents have traditionally had little interaction with tourists to the sanctuary. However, they are starting to offer some tourist services, including room and board for visitors. Early rising birdwatchers are taking advantage of this service. Horse owners have begun renting horses for riding, and boat owners are giving boat trips.

There has also been a substantial economic impact from tourism at the Bermudian Landing Howler Reserve. With the completion of the visitor center, and the guide service provided there, the residents are receiving income from tourists. With construction of the anticipated bed and breakfast, tourism is expected to become an even bigger source of local income.

B. Environmental Impacts of Nature Tourism

1. Conservation Activities and Environmental Education

Many benefits have resulted from increased tourism in Belize, some by an indirect route. One notable example is the

Hol Chan Marine Reserve, which was recently established to control diving and fishing in order to sustain the area's resources. Hol Chan was established when local residents solicited the support of the Belizean government and the international conservation community to protect part of the barrier reef that was being destroyed because of uncontrolled tourism. The declaration of this protected area and the consequent conservation of the marine resources, will allow the area to support a sustainable tourism industry.

Other impacts of the nature tourism business on conservation efforts can be seen in the large number of naturalists and conservationists who are involved with nature tourism accommodations or guide services. For example, some board members and employees of the BAS also own hotels or tour operator services. Also, in addition, the head of the Cockscomb Jaguar Sanctuary Committee is also the manager of the nearby Pelican Beach Hotel.

Nature tourists have also raised the level of environmental awareness in the country. International tourists coming to see the natural resources of Belize have given a new value to these resources for nationals. Also, the Belize Zoo has been conducting an extensive environmental education program for visitors to the zoo as well as for local communities.

2. Negative Environmental Impacts

To date, environmental problems due to tourism have been minimal. There have been some reports of tourists destroying coral formations at Hol Chan, and reports of litter in other areas. If these problems are not monitored, they will become more serious; however, they are at present under control. In giving a status report on environmental impacts, it is important to note that thorough scientific studies of environmental carrying capacities have yet to be conducted for any protected area in Belize.

C. Sociocultural Considerations

Sociocultural issues were not a focal point for this study, and therefore no conclusions are presented. However, sociocultural considerations are essential when developing and managing protected areas for tourism.

IV. Obstacles and Opportunities for Growth of Nature Tourism

A. Obstacles for Growth

One constraint to the growth of nature tourism in Belize is the lack of or poor condition of infrastructure for tourists. Many of the roads in the interior of Belize are rough, and some are impassable during rainy season. Until recently, most accommodations were concentrated in Belize City (35 percent) and the Cayes (31 percent), requiring most ventures into interior protected areas to be just one-day trips. Several small lodges near protected areas--such as the Chaa Creek Cottages and the Rio Bravo development--have just been completed.

Another constraint to tourism expansion is inadequate international and national promotion. Aside from some scuba-diving areas that have been promoted by private investors, many of Belize's protected areas remain largely unknown. Promotion efforts are increasing, but many people still know very little about the country.

The lack of a park service in Belize has also constrained tourism to protected area resources. Although protected areas are being managed, there has been no single agency with the responsibility for developing park management plans and actually monitoring and promoting the parks and reserves.

B. Opportunities for Growth

Belize is in a good position to develop its nature tourism industry. First of all, its natural environment is virtually intact and there is relatively little destruction in its resources. Secondly, the present administration is very interested in promoting tourism to protected areas and will lend support to the industry. Thirdly, Belize is close to two big markets for nature tourists, the United States and Canada. Finally, as an English-speaking country in Central America, Belize attracts English-speaking people who do not want to confront a foreign language. These are all important factors that can contribute to the success of the nature tourism industry and make the development of this industry a timely endeavor now.

V. Cockscomb Basin Wildlife Sanctuary (Case Study #1)

A. General Description and Infrastructure

In 1986, the Belizean government set aside a portion of the Cockscomb Forest Reserve as a sanctuary to protect prime jaguar habitat. The Cockscomb Jaguar Sanctuary is a 1,417 hectare (3,500-acre) site that hosts not only jaguars, but also populations of wildlife species such as the endangered ocelot, margay, baird's tapir (the national animal), white-lipped and collared peccary, scarlet macaw, tayra, otter, coati, kinkajou, brocket deer, agouti, paca, anteater, and armadillo. Additionally, the sanctuary is very popular with birdwatchers. Species to be found there include the toucan, the king vulture, and the curassow.

Cockscomb Basin Wildlife Sanctuary is 11.3 kilometers (7 miles) off the Southern Highway on an unpaved road. Even in dry season, a four-wheel-drive vehicle is recommended for traveling the road. During rainy season, the road is subject to flooding and visits to the sanctuary are problematic if not impossible.

Cockscomb is managed by the Belize Audubon Society. In the last few years, BAS has overseen the rapid development of basic infrastructure. The sanctuary now has simple accommodations consisting of two cabins with room for 10 people, and latrines. Recently, a potable water system has been finished. Overnight visitors pay a minimal fee, and differential rates are charged for foreigners, nationals, and children.

Additional infrastructure includes a visitor center, a picnic area, and several marked routes and jungle trails. A large map of the park is available, as are interpretive brochures with descriptions about the park's flora and fauna.

Funding for Cockcomb's infrastructure development comes mainly from international funding organizations. However, revenues from tourism are increasing and are expected to make a bigger contribution to park maintenance in the future.

B. Visitor Information to Date

Visitation statistics have been recorded only since November of 1986 and show the following monthly distribution:

Table 3.

VISITORS TO COCKSCOMB BASIN WILDLIFE SANCTUARY
1986-1988

MONTH	1986	1987	1988
January		63	102
February		79	49
March		96	48
April		117	168
May		131	179
June		152	186
July		107	45
August		62	n/a
September		41	n/a
October		49	n/a
November	42	88	n/a
December	48	113	n/a
Total	90	1,098	777
			(incomplete)

Source: Cockscomb Sanctuary visitor book, August 1988

Based on these available statistics, it is difficult to establish a trend. However April, May, and June of 1988 did show an increase in visitors over the same months in 1987.

C. WWF Park Survey Results

1. Visitor Profile

Further data on visitor patterns and profiles were obtained during our two survey weeks[1], when 42 international visitors were interviewed. With the exception of one (Japanese), all visitors were North American. The majority were male (67 percent) and came with friends or colleagues (57 percent) or with relatives (19 percent). About 19 percent indicated that they came with a tour group. In most cases (75 percent), the excursion to Cockscomb had been planned beforehand; the remaining visitors (25 percent) had spontaneously followed local advice.

---

[1]One week in February (high season), and one week in May (low season)

19

It should be noted that there are many Europeans who visit Cockscomb, and this survey is not necessarily representative of all visitors.

Among the list of motivations to visit the park, the most frequently cited reasons were its fauna (81 percent), and to a lesser extent, adventure (21 percent).

Visitors arrived by automobile (71 percent), or by bus (26 percent). About one-fourth of all visitors indicated that they had spent the night in one of the preserve's two lodges. Over 50 percent said they had spent the night in a good quality local hotel or a pension outside of the preserve, most likely in Dangriga. The mean number of nights spent in or near the park was 1.9.

2. Visitor Impressions

Visitors' impressions of the sanctuary as a tourist attraction were also obtained in the WWF park survey. Over 84 percent of interviewed tourists described their park experience as excellent or good. While a majority (78 percent) considered the park's infrastructure and installations to be excellent or good, about 20 percent described them as mediocre.

Visitors enjoyed Cockscomb's natural features, especially its flora, and praised the park guards and manager. Many expressed displeasure with the access roads, the price of lodging, the lack of an interpretive center, and the lack of food at the sanctuary.

Asked for suggestions how to improve the park experience, visitors recommended road improvements, technical information on the area, more maps of the area, and improved toilet facilities.

D. Economic Impacts of Tourism at Cockscomb Sanctuary

Local economic impacts have thus far been small because of the location of the preserve and low annual visitation figures. However, some interesting developments in the local community, Maya Center, have occurred. When tourists began coming to the preserve, the local women recognized the demand for souvenirs. They began selling beads at the entry gate and recently have joined in a cooperative gift shop. Although the shop has been open for only a few months, it has already achieved satisfactory financial gains. Several young people are being trained as tour guides. These activities have brought some economic returns to the villagers. At present, no one locally has expressed an interest in establishing hotel facilities since the Belize

Audubon Society already has built the two cabins inside the preserve. Many park visitors stay in the nearest town, Dangriga. One of the hotels in this town offers day trips to the sanctuary.

E. Environmental Impacts

Environmental impacts thus far have been minimal. The small-scale economic activity derived from tourism apparently has positively encouraged the local population to "protect" the park. It has also been reported by the Cockscomb staff that some larger mammals have shown an increased presence in the sanctuary.

VI. Crooked Tree Wildlife Sanctuary (Case Study #2)

A. General Description and Infrastructure

Crooked Tree is located about 35 miles northwest of Belize City. It is 2 miles off the main highway and can be reached by a causeway, completed two years ago, that crosses an inland lagoon to the sanctuary. Established in 1984 for the protection of resident and migrant birds, the sanctuary consists of a network of inland lagoons, swamps, and waterways. During the dry season, thousands of birds congregate at Crooked Tree to take advantage of the food resources and find a nesting spot on their spring migration back to the north. Animals found within the Sanctuary include the boat-billed heron, chestnut-bellied heron, black-collared hawks, black howler monkeys, and the morelet's crocodiles.

There is a modest but informative visitor center at the sanctuary. The area's flora and fauna are displayed in the center, and brochures are available about the sanctuary. The sanctuary has three employees: one Peace Corps volunteer and two park wardens.

The village of Crooked Tree, next to the sanctuary, has thus far had little interaction with tourists. The village was established during the logwood era in Belizean history. The main economic activities of the village population are agriculture--specifically, cashew and mango--and fishing. With the recent opening of the causeway, many residents are finding employment outside of the village.

B. Visitor Information to Date

Visitation statistics are available only since October of 1986, but they clearly demonstrate the increase of tourism to the park:

Table 4.

_____

VISITATION AT CROOKED TREE WILDLIFE SANCTUARY
1986 - 1988

MONTH	1986	1987	1988
January		33	133
February		69	177
March		51	127
April		49	80
May		19	24
June		37	45
July		21	n/a
August		38	n/a
September		8	n/a
October	9	40	n/a
November	10	64	n/a
December		129	n/a
Total	19	558	586
			(incomplete)

Source: Crooked Tree Visitors Book, 1987/88

_____

C. WWF Park Survey Results

1. Visitor Profile

Specific information on visitor patterns and profiles was obtained during our two survey weeks, when a total of 39 international visitors were interviewed.[2] With the exception of two (Europeans), all interviewed visitors were North Americans. Over half of the visitors were male, the mean age being 49.1. The mean income of visitors was close to U.S. $40,000 per year. Most visitors came with relatives to the park (49 percent) or were accompanied by friends and colleagues (33 percent). About 28 percent stated that they came with a tour group. In most cases, the excursion to the sanctuary had been planned before arriving in Belize. However, about one-third decided during their stay in Belize to visit the sanctuary, mainly based upon recommendations from friends or from brochures in the country.

_____

[2]one week in high season (February)
one week in low season (May)

23

The main motivation to visit Crooked Tree is its fauna (59 percent) and recreation (28 percent). While in the sanctuary, primary tourist activities were birdwatching and wildlife observation.

Visitors arrived by automobile (62 percent) or bus (33 percent). No visitor spent the night in the sanctuary, but over one-third indicated that they stayed overnight in a good quality hotel outside of sanctuary. The mean number of nights spent near Crooked Tree was 1.5.

2. Visitor Impressions

Visitors' impressions of Crooked Tree as a tourist attraction can be obtained from the WWF park survey. All visitors described their excursion to the sanctuary as either good (64 percent) or excellent (36 percent), and an overwhelming majority was equally satisfied with the sanctuary's infrastructure and installations.

Visitors enjoyed the sanctuary's natural features and birdwatching opportunities. They praised the sanctuary guards and managers. Few mentioned dislikes, but the ones mentioned included difficulties in reaching the sanctuary, guide services, lack of food, water quality, and the interpretive center.

When asked for improvements needed to enhance the experience of visiting the sanctuary, visitors suggested guidebooks, technical information, an improved road system, and improved guide services.

D. Economic Impacts of Tourism to Crooked Tree

The increase of tourists to Crooked Tree is starting to expand the economic opportunities of the local population. Some families are providing room and food for visitors staying for a few days; horse owners rent horses for horseback riding; boat owners rent boats for trips up and down the lagoons; the sale of beverages to visitors has been increasing; and local women are selling needlework to visitors.

E. Environmental Impacts of Tourism to Crooked Tree

Environmental impacts have thus far not been reported, however, comprehensive environmental studies have yet to be conducted.

CHAPTER 2

COSTA RICA

I. Status of Tourism Industry

A. History and Growth

Costa Rica has recognized the importance of tourism to its economy for many years, but it is only recently that the country has become a well-known tourist destination. With the establishment of an outstanding system of parks and reserves, the natural resources of Costa Rica are receiving worldwide attention, and the tourism industry is now increasing its efforts to promote nature tourism.

Costa Rica's first national tourist board, the Junta Nacional de Turismo, was set up in 1931. The board was replaced by the Costa Rican Tourist Board (ICT) in 1955. Foreign tourism grew most rapidly in the 1970s, when growth averaged 11.2 percent annually. (The Economist, 1987). At this time, tourism became the third largest source of income, behind banana and coffee export, in Costa Rica (Table 1). Tourism has not only maintained its position as third leading earner, but also has had the largest percentage increase among all other foreign exchange earners in the last decade. In 1986, tourism represented 16 percent of the country's total foreign exchange.

Table 1.

VALUE OF COSTA RICAN EXPORTS
1979 - 1986

	1979	1980	1981	1982	1983	1984	1985	1986
Coffee	315.4	257.9	240.0	236.9	229.9	264.6	308.9	371.8
Bananas	190.5	207.5	244.8	228.1	240.3	229.4	201.4	228.2
Tourism	72.7	84.4	93.6	131.1	130.6	117.3	118.3	132.7
Meat	82.5	71.8	76.5	53.1	31.9	46.9	52.5	66.2
Sugar	17.5	40.7	42.0	16.6	23.8	29.2	10.5	18.5
Fertilizers	9.3	10.0	15.6	7.9	5.5	5.6	7.6	4.7
Cocoa	9.7	4.2	2.7	2.4	0.9	1.0	- - -	- - -

Source: Chaverri, 1988

25

For many years, Costa Rica has been known for peace and democracy, a high level of education and health care, and stable, pleasant weather. Traditionally, tourism has been concentrated around San Jose, the capital, in the central highlands. However, tour operators soon realized that the city could not compete with other capital cities that offered more museums, commercial areas, entertainment and nightlife. Therefore, tour operators began promoting what is unique in Costa Rica--a network of natural protected areas that hold an immense diversity of wildlife and wildlands.

Tourist statistics in Costa Rica show that the number of visitor arrivals has alternately risen and fallen during the last decade. There were 299,039 visitor arrivals in 1976, with steady increases to a peak of 340,442 in 1978. The 1979 revolution in neighboring Nicaragua affected Costa Rica's tourism and brought arrivals down to 317,724. Numbers began to rise again, reaching 371,582 in 1982. The main reason for this second peak year was the increase in Central American visitors, primarily Panamanians, perhaps because of a favorable exchange rate. Then, with further trouble in the region, numbers fell to 326,142 in 1983, then to 273,901 in 1984; they continued to decline for the next couple of years.

Traditionally, most of Costa Rica's tourists were from other Central American countries, particularly Nicaragua, which accounted for 36.7 percent of all international tourist arrivals in 1978. However, the percentage of Central American visitors has fallen in the last decade overall. The European and North American portion of the market has varied somewhat, but has been rising overall in the same time period.

Political and economic difficulties in Central America have affected tourism in Costa Rica in various ways. Certainly they have contributed to the decline in the number of Central Americans who travel to Costa Rica for vacation, but the impact of these difficulties on tourism by other international visitors is less clear. For people outside Central America, changes in tourism patterns can be attributed to variances in perception of how closely Costa Rica is tied to danger in Central America or to what extent Costa Rica is seen as a distinct and peaceful country in the midst of violence.

Visitor expenditures have risen consistently in the last decade, with only one exception in 1984-85. Expenditures have risen from U.S. $57,062,105 in 1976 to $132,700,000 in 1986. Of the total for 1986, North Americans accounted for 44 percent, Central Americans for 29 percent, Europeans for 12 percent, South Americans for 9 percent, Caribbeans for 1% and all others for about 5 percent. It is estimated that the economic multiplier of tourism income in Costa Rica is between 3.2 and 5.5 (Chaverri, 1988).

B. Major Tourism Attractions

Costa Rica is a small country, roughly 52,000 square kilometers. Despite its small size, however, Costa Rica comprises an enormous variety of topography, climate, and plant and animal life. The temperature changes with altitude, and rainfall and humidity vary greatly with distance from the oceans or the mountains. Geographically, the country is a bridge between two continents, with species migration between North and South America that has produced a spectacularly diverse wildlife.

The country has four mountain ranges, two of which are of volcanic origin. It contains large tracts of tropical rain forest and other endangered ecosystems. Costa Rica has dry tropical forests, cloud forests, mountain paramos, mangroves, white and black sand beaches, coral reefs, volcanoes, and a number of other natural attractions that are playing an increasingly important role in the development of tourism in Costa Rica.

Many of these natural attractions are under some form of protection. The Costa Rican Parks System covers nearly 20 percent of the country, with 19 national parks and reserves and several other private parks. The Parks System encompasses representative samples of nearly all habitats and most of the 1,500 distinct species of trees, 850 birds, and over 6,000 kinds of flowering plants in Costa Rica, including 1,500 varieties of orchids. The most visited parks are Poás Volcano National Park, Cahuita, Manuel Antonio, Irazú Volcano, Santa Rosa, Tortuguero, Corcovado, and Carara.

The beach resorts of Costa Rica, almost all on the Pacific shore, are not as fully developed as the beach resorts of the Caribbean or of Mexico. With few exceptions, Costa Rican beach resorts are small and do not draw as many tourists as those of other countries in the region.

Tourists are also attracted to visit San Jose, the capital of Costa Rica, with its modern airport, good hotels, restaurants, and tourist information centers. Other attractions include the National Museum, with its displays of the country's flora, fauna, and history; the National Insurance Institute, which houses a large exhibit of jade and ceramics; the Metropolitan Cathedral; the Museum of Costa Rican Art, and the National Artisan Market. The city has no national convention center, although many conventions are held at hotels.

27

C. Tourism Policy, Management, and Promotion

During the 1970s and early 1980s, tourism was not regarded as a priority sector by the government, and the tourism board (ICT) did not receive much attention or funding. While the manufacturing sector had been receiving preferential interest rates, tourism development was minimal. However, in the 1980s, manufacturing investment began to stagnate, and the tourist industry to decline. With this situation, the government decided that tourism should become a national priority; it allocated more funds for the tourism board and also declared preferential interest rates for tourism. In 1986, the government passed the "Law of Tourism Incentives" to demonstrate its commitment to developing the tourism industry.

The current government, which took power in 1986, is also focusing a great deal of attention on tourism and is reorganizing the tourism board. In 1986, the government continued the practice initiated in 1985 of increasing the tourism board's budget from central funds and also increased the tax on airfares from 5 percent to 8 percent to increase the board's funding. This airfare tax and a 3 percent tax on hotel accommodation are intended to fund the board totally (The Economist, 1987). Also, the government would like to add 2,000 new hotel rooms by the 1990s.

As indicated in the Tourism Development Strategy for 1984-90, the trend in tourism policy in Costa Rica is toward specialized tourism. The ITC has identified four areas to be developed in the tourism sector over the next five years. These are: nature and adventure tourism, sun and beach tourism, cruise ship tourism, and convention or business tourism.

As outlined in the strategy, one of the primary efforts of tourism promotion will be to encourage "soft" nature tourism through day trips to parks. Also identified in the strategy are infrastructure priorities, such as improvements in domestic air services and completion of the roads from San Jose to the Caribbean and Pacific coasts.

The ITC conducted visitor surveys in 1985, 1986, and 1987 to determine main visitor motivation factors. The term "ecotourism" did not appear on the 1985 survey, but was introduced in 1986. The fact that about 36 percent of the visitors included "ecotourism" among their main reasons for visiting Costa Rica is no doubt significant (Table 2).

28

Table 2.

MAJOR/MAIN MOTIVATIONS FOR TOURIST TRAVEL TO COSTA RICA

	1985			1986	1987
Weather	23.0%		Natural	87.0%	72.3%
Beaches	23.0%		beauty		
Nature	9.5%		Culture	78.1%	66.8%
Democracy			Fishing		
and peace	9.0%		and sports	16.7%	13.9%
Cheap country	6.0%		Ecotourism	35.9%	36.1%
People	5.5%		Other	21.4%	
Other	24.0%				

Source: Costa Rican Board of Tourism Survey 1985, 1986, 1987

Within the country, there are two major vehicles for promotion of Costa Rica as a tourist destination. In addition to the ICT, there is also an annual trade fair. Started in 1985, Expotur, is financed by the country's trade associations. The most active tourism associations are Canatur, the national tourism chamber to which all sectors of industry and regional tourism chambers belong, and ACRPROT, the travel agencies association.

II. Status of Tourism to Protected Areas

A. Demand for Tourism to Protected Areas

The increasing demand for nature tourism in Costa Rica is reflected in the increasing number of tour operators who are offering tours to protected areas. Of the approximately 30 travel agencies in Costa Rica, one-third are called "ecotourism agencies." Examples of these agencies are Costa Rica Expeditions, founded in 1979, Tikal (1983), Horizontes (1984), Geotour (1985), Interviajes (1985), and Cosmos (1986).

Other travel groups that do not specialize in "ecotourism travel" also offer trips to protected areas. For example, Blanco and Swiss travel agencies sporadically arrange natural history tours. Mawamba offers tours specifically to Tortuguero Park. Marenco is a private reserve with its own travel agency. The Organization for Tropical States brings visitors to its three biological stations (La Selva, Palo Verde, and Wilson Gardens). The Tropical Science Center coordinates tours to Monteverde Reserve.

Demand for tourism to protected areas can also be seen in the following table of the number of foreign visitors to national parks between 1981 and 1986.

Table 3.

NUMBER OF FOREIGN VISITORS TO NATIONAL PARKS AND RESERVES
IN COSTA RICA, 1981 - 1986

NATIONAL PARK	1981	1982	1983	1984	1986	TOTAL	PERCENT
Volcan Poas	10,898	17,934	22,593	23,380	24,640	98,445	31.1
Volcan Irazu	17,094	26,321	19,162	20,839	18,597	102,013	32.5
Manuel Antonio	7,790	13,690	12,435	11,027	16,234	61,176	19.5
Cahuita	2,657	4,369	3,559	5,270	8,383	24,238	7.7
Monteverde	2,127	2,827	4,539	4,090		13,583	4.3
Santa Rosa	851	1,255	1,347	1,343	1,161	5,957	1.9
Guayabo	494	471	314	403	464	2,146	0.7
Braulio Carrillo	103	64	77	255		499	0.2
Tortuguero	296	448	139	843	1,032	2,758	0.9
Chirripo	76	179	53	118	166	592	0.2
Barra Honda	30	75	25	103	57	290	0.1
Corcovado	357	265	415	261	59	1,357	0.4
Rincon de la Vieja	124	114	147	114	164	663	0.2
Santa Ana	242	193				435	0.2
Cabo Blanco					99	99	0.0
Total	43,109	68,130	64,780	67,943	69,999	313,961	100

Source: National Park Service (NPS)

Surveys were conducted at the airport in San Jose to determine the degree to which natural protected areas influenced tourists' travel plans and activities. First, socio-demographic information was collected, and then visitors were asked how important protected areas were in their decision to visit the country, how many protected areas they visited, and what kinds of nature-oriented activities they participated in during their trip.

WWF Airport Survey Results

Socio-demographic Information

Average age: 39.5 years, youngest 21, oldest 75 years old (N=82).

Average nights: Average number of nights was 15.6; shortest stay was overnight, longest was 99+ (N=96).

Family members: Of the 104 tourists surveyed, 30 (29 percent) came with family members. Average was 2.8 people, or closer to three total family members. The largest family had eight members.

Expenditures: Average total trip expenditures in Costa Rica were $1,311 (N=96), for an average daily expenditure of $131 per day. The highest total expenditure for any tourist was over $9,999 and the cheapest vacation cost $40. Of the 96 people responding to this question, 48 people reported an average expenditure of $782 for airfare.

Income: The average family income range was between $30,000 and $40,000.

Gender: 66 percent of respondents were men, 31 percent were women, and 3 percent gave no response concerning gender.

Nationality: The nationality distribution of the survey respondents (N=104) was as follows: 51.0 percent North American, 28.8 percent European, 2.9 percent Panamanian, 2.9 percent Colombian, and 14.4 percent all other.

Protected Area and Nature-oriented Tourism

Parks and protected areas were important in the tourists' decisions to visit Costa Rica:

Main reason	14%
Important, influenced decision	27%
Somewhat important	17%
Not important	36%

No response   6%

Many of the tourists to Costa Rica had been there before;
41 percent had previously visited the country, while for 57
percent it was their first trip (2 percent gave no response).
The top five reasons given to visit Costa Rica were:

Visit friends or family   35%
Natural history   30%
Sun/beaches/recreation   30%
Sightseeing   28%
Business   24%

The activities most commonly enjoyed by all tourists
interviewed were nature based activities. Although tourists
expressed multiple responses, it is important that a high
percentage, no matter what their reason for travel to the
country, participated in nature-based activities:

Wildlife observing   37%
Jungle excursions   33%
Birdwatching   31%
Boat trips   25%
Botany   18%
Hiking/trekking   16%
Local cultures   14%
Hunting/fishing   12%
Camping   10%
Mountaineering   9%

When asked to list what they liked most about Costa Rica, 45
of 104 surveyed listed the "friendliness of the people." Both
the "climate" and Costa Rica's "natural features and beauty"
were highlighted by 26 visitors. Also mentioned were the
country's "parks and protected areas," listed by 17 visitors; 11
visitors listed the "food and restaurants" of Costa Rica. The
most frequently listed dislike, 27 out of 104, was the country's
"pollution, noise, and litter." Twelve visitors listed the
"downtown area of San Jose" as a dislike.

33

B. Supply of Protected Areas

1. Development and Management of Park System

The park system in Costa Rica developed primarily through the efforts of biologists and other conservationists concerned about depletion of the forests. The country had extensive tropical forests until the late 1940s. Within 30 years, many of these forests were lost. In the late 1960s, a small movement began to protect what was left of Costa Rica's natural heritage. This led to creation of the National Parks Service in 1970, under the direction of the Ministry of Agriculture and Livestock.

Costa Rica had just a few parks and reserves in 1970. However, by 1987, the nation had over 55 protected units, such as national parks, national forests, wildlife refuges, and Indian reserves. These areas cover about 18 percent (926,000 hectares) of the national territory.

The wildlands of Costa Rica provide shelter for most of the 12,000 species of plants, 237 species of mammals, 848 species of birds, and 361 species of amphibians and reptiles that have been identified in the country. They also conserve almost all the existing natural habitat types, such as deciduous forests, mangrove swamps, rain forests, marshes, paramos, cloud forests, coral reefs, riparian forests, and swamp forests (Boza, 1986).

The National Park Service is the agency that has been in charge of managing the majority of the protected units. It employs approximately 350 individuals. Employees all receive some level of training, ranging from week-long workshops to full-length graduate programs. The National Forest Service and the Department of Wildlife and Fisheries have also managed some areas.

In 1989, the protected area system was reorganized under a new umbrella agency that will manage all national parks, national forests, national wildlife refuges, and Indian reserves. Under this new system, nine protected area units have been designed, each containing numerous parks and reserves, for a new management scheme.

2. Examples of Protected Areas

Santa Rosa National Park

Santa Rosa, a national park of 21,913 hectares, is important for two reasons. Historically, it was the scene of the Battle of Santa Rosa in 1856, one of the major heroic feats in the national history of Costa Rica. Ecologically, it is an integral area in the protection of the climatic zone known as the "Dry Pacific." For this reason, and because of its great biological variety--603 types of plant species, 75 species of mammals, 260 bird species, and an extraordinary number of insect species--Santa Rosa has become an important international research center for ecological studies of dry tropical forests.

Carara Biological Reserve

A transition zone between a dry region to the north and a more humid region to the south, Carara, a biological reserve of 4,700 hectares, is considered a veritable oasis due to its great variety of plant life as well as its many different aquatic habitats, including swamps, several streams, and a lagoon with floating vegetation. Additionally, the reserve offers an archeological site (a cemetery) in Lomas Carara.

Manuel Antonio Natural Park

Renowned for its beauty, Manuel Antonio Natural Park's main attractions are its two white-sand beaches, which are rimmed by tall evergreen forests and slope gently down to transparent blue water. Twelve islands lie just off the coast of the park, providing refuge for sea birds as well as an important nesting ground for the brown booby. Terrestrial wildlife is varied--109 species of mammals and 184 species of birds--but the marine flora and fauna are particularly diverse. Most notably, 10 species of sponges, 19 of coral, 24 of crustaceans, 17 of seaweed, and 78 of fish have been identified in the six main sea habitats. The park, which is 690 hectares in size, also offers three geological attractions: a sand bar, a blow-hole, and sea caves along Serrucho Point.

Corcovado National Park

Located in one of the rainiest regions of the country, Corcovado's 41,788 hectares host about 500 species of trees, some of which are giants reaching heights of 50 meters. An extraordinarily diverse wildlife includes 300 species of birds, 139 of mammals, and 116 of amphibians and reptiles identified to date. It is estimated that 5,000 to 10,000 species of insects are to be found within the boundaries of the park alone. Corcovado protects the largest population of scarlet macaw in Costa Rica, as well as endangered species such as the jaguar, crocodile, and tapir. Because of its geographic location and impressive diversity of wildlife, the park has become an important international center for tropical rain forest research.

Braulio Carrillo National Park

Braulio Carrillo's drastic topographic variations, consisting of high mountains, deep canyons, and rushing rivers, combined with high precipitation levels, result in an infinite number of waterfalls in the park. Other impressive geographic features within its 31,401 hectares include two extinct volcanoes and several lakes. The park enjoys an abundance of flora and fauna, notably 6,000 plant species and 400 species of birds. A modern highway crosses this park.

Poás Volcano National Park

The most developed and visited park in Costa Rica, Poás is widely considered to hold one of the most spectacular active volcanoes in the country--its enormous mouth measures 1.5 kilometers in diameter and 300 meters deep. Eruptions of the volcano spew immense columns of muddy water and steam, sometimes to heights of 200 meters. Such eruptions have earned Poás the distinction of being the largest geyser in the world. The park covers 5,317 hectares and contains little wildlife, although many birds can be found, particularly hummingbirds and sooty robins.

Irazú Volcano National Park

Known as "the deadly powder keg of nature," Irazú is an active volcano with a long history of eruptions of burning rock and ash. Present activity, however, has been reduced to moderate emissions of gases and vapors. The violence of Irazú's past eruptions is nevertheless reflected in the park's sparse and twisted vegetation and scarcity of wildlife over its 2,398 hectares. On clear days it is possible to see both oceans from Irazú's summit.

Tortuguero National Park

Tortuguero, one of the rainiest regions in the country, is also considered to be one of the most ecological diverse wildlands. Because of the dense vegetation and swampy terrain, however, the park's rich wildlife is difficult to observe. The park is 18,946 hectares in size, and as indicated by its name, is known for the species of sea turtles that come to nest there, most notably the green turtle, leatherback turtle, and hawksbill turtle. Part of Tortuguero's scenic beauty is the natural system of lakes and navigable canals crossing the park, which form the habitat for two endangered species--the crocodile and the West Indian manatee.

Cahuita National Park

The beauty of Cahuita is best seen in its long white beaches, crystal clear water, and coral reef covering an expanse of 600 hectares. The only well-preserved reef along the Costa Rican Caribbean coast, it holds 35 species of coral, 140 of mollusks, 44 of crustaceans, 128 of seaweed, and 500 of fish. Wildlife in this park is varied--it is common to see crabs, howler monkeys, racoons, and several species of swamp forest birds--and habitats range from dry mixed forest, mangrove swamp, and littoral woodland covering an area of 1,067 hectares. One unique attraction to Cahuita is the ruins of a shipwreck just off the coast, dating from the 18th century.

III. Impacts of Tourism to Protected Areas

A. Economic Activities Related to Nature Tourism

While there are no comprehensive statistics on the economic impact of nature tourism as a subsector of tourism, there are several means to measure the economic activities related to nature tourism. One way is to quantify the activities of tour operators to protected areas who are directly involved with the industry. Another way is to look at specific protected area sites and quantify the extent of economic activity related to tourists.

Monteverde Cloud Forest Reserve

Monteverde is a private reserve that is experiencing a boom in tourism in recent years. The number of tourists increased from about 300 in 1973 to nearly 13,000 in 1987. The economic impact of this expansion has been substantial.

One important source of tourist income has been entrance fees. Entrance fees at Monteverde are higher than at most other public parks in Costa Rica (roughly U.S. $2.75 vs. $.65). This income has covered maintenance costs of the park in the last few years. Table 4 shows park expenses and entrance fee income for 1983-87. In 1987, 68 percent of total expenses was for personnel, 13 percent for maintenance, 15 percent for services, and 4 percent for tax and other purposes.

Table 4.

ANNUAL INCOME AND EXPENSES
MONTEVERDE CLOUD FOREST RESERVE 1983 - 1987

YEAR	EXPENSES (in colones)	INCOME (in colones)
1983	850,000	1,000,000
1984	950,000	1,250,000
1985	1,399,000	1,335,707
1986	1,375,364	2,181,025
1987	2,676,393	2,740,629
TOTAL	7,250,757	8,507,362

Source: Monteverde Cloud Forest Reserve, 1988

Tourism has also had an enormous economic impact within the community surrounding the reserve. Tourism earnings are the second largest source of income for local residents after dairy production. Much infrastructure has been developed for tourists, which has consequently increased the number of people employed in tourist-related activities. Today there are two hotels, two pensions, a souvenir and crafts store, horse rentals, and the most recent additions, a disco-bar and a cantina.

The four lodging places have a total of 48 rooms, with a daily capacity of 152 guests. Occupancy at all places is very seasonal. Permanent employment at the accommodation facilities is low. In addition to the owners, who often work at the hotels, the Hotel de Montana has nine employees, Quetzal has three, Flor Mar has two, and Belmar has three. However, during high tourist season, employment rates grow to 14 at Hotel de Montaña, 6 at Quetzal, 5 at Flor Mar and 9 at Belmar. Salaries in these facilities are higher than the regional average. (Frueh, 1988)

The souvenir and crafts shop is a very profitable enterprise, with annual sales recently reaching U.S. $50,000. The shop was founded in 1982 by eight women as a cooperative venture. With the increasing numbers of tourists and the demand for souvenirs from the area, the founders established a Coop called CASEM (Cooperative de Artesanos de Santa Elena y Monteverde). CASEM now has 70 members, primarily women. The members produce and sell embroidered shirts and dresses, painted shirts and hats, ceramic and wood-carved souvenirs, and other items. Sales doubled between 1987 and 1988 (Frueh, 1988).

Tourism has also increased the demand for guides. While some guides come in with tour groups from San Jose, many local residents also have become independent guides. Two residents make their primary income as nature guides. In addition, a few locals have been hired directly by travel agencies that bring groups to Monteverde.

In terms of indirect economic benefits, local agriculturalists have not experienced a great increase in demand for their products because of tourism. Aside from local dairy products, which are of very high quality and are used widely at tourist facilities, most other agricultural goods are not produced in the area and are brought in from nearby large towns, such as Puntarenas and Canas.

Currently there is much debate among Monteverde residents about the economic impact of tourism. While it is clearly a significant and growing source of income for the area, there are concerns about such impact. Residents want to ensure that tourism remains small-scale and that benefits are not concentrated in too few hands. Residents are also concerned that increasing recognition of their area is driving up land prices. Escalating real estate costs have put land around Monteverde among the highest costs per hectare in Costa Rica, and these costs are straining agricultural expansion. The tourism boom in this area is thus seen as a mixed blessing.

Volcan Poas National Park

Volcan Poas is located 60 kilometers from San Jose. As with many parks that are located close to a large city, the economic impact of tourism to Poas is minimal to the nearby surrounding residents. Despite high visitation figures, there is little demand for overnight facilities at Poas. The only overnight facility is a designated camping area that receives few campers.

On the road to Poas are a few restaurants and cafes, totalling just over 300 seats. There are three pensions and one souvenir store. Employment at the restaurants is about 16 people during the week and double that number on weekends. On weekends, there are also a number of street vendors, most of them selling strawberries. For the majority of people involved with these enterprises, tourism revenue is not their primary source of income.

At the park itself, income generation is even less than on the road to the park. A small entrance fee is collected that covers some of the park maintenance costs. There is a small visitor center, but no other tourism infrastructure, such as a snack bar or souvenir shop. Therefore, the revenue generated at the park is very limited.

B. Positive and Negative Environmental Impacts

1. Conservation Activities and Environmental Education

Nature tourism has had many positive impacts in Costa Rica. The recent creation of several parks can be attributed, at least partially, to the need to create more tourism opportunities in the country. Manuel Antonio and Cahuita Parks are examples of this. Nature tourism in general has given conservationists an "economic" argument for protecting resources.

In some cases, increased funding for Costa Rican conservation activities and for park management results directly from tourists who have visited and been impressed by protected areas. The Monteverde Conservation League has received approximately 50 percent of its funds from tourists who have visited Monteverde Reserve and wanted to make a contribution to its protection.

Environmental education has also received a boost from nature tourists. Many visitors centers have been built at parks and reserves with interpretive displays of the local natural resources. Poas has one of the better known visitor centers, with many informative exhibits about the wildlife and wildlands of the region.

2. Negative Environmental Impacts

While there have been few serious environmental problems recorded to date, there have not yet been any comprehensive scientific studies of the environmental impacts of nature tourism. Therefore, the only available information is through observation. People have reported some environmental problems at Monteverde and Poas. At Monteverde, there are reports of trail erosion, especially during rainy season, due to tourists. At Poas, many people have noted extensive litter, especially on the weekends.

C. Sociocultural Considerations

Sociocultural issues were not a focus of this study, and therefore, a complete analysis is not presented. However, sociocultural considerations are an essential component of nature tourism development and need to be further studied.

The importance of sociocultural considerations in tourism development can be seen in the example of the Monteverde community. Facing increasing tourism, local residents have been concerned with maintaining control over the tourism so that it does not disrupt their community life. They are concerned that the benefits of tourism may become concentrated in the hands of too few people and negatively affect the structure of their society.

Another case in which sociocultural considerations have already emerged is Carara Reserve. Resentment has been building among the residents of nearby Tarcoles and Bijagual since the recent establishment of the reserve. The reserve has limited their access to a zone in which they traditionally habitually hunted or searched for indigenous artifacts. Tension has been rising between the community and park personnel, and could affect tourism to the park. (Frueh, 1988)

IV. Obstacles and Opportunities for Growth in Nature Tourism

A. Obstacles for Growth

At this time, the primary obstacle to the growth of tourism in Costa Rica is inadequate infrastructure in some parks and reserves. One problem that may be contributing to the lack of infrastructure is that parks do not currently generate enough money from tourism for park maintenance. National parks charge a nominal entrance fee that does not cover maintenance costs. Eventually, poor maintenance of the parks will have a negative effect on the number of visitors to the park.

B. Opportunities for Growth

Costa Rica has many factors in its favor to develop the nature tourism industry. The national park system offers many distinctive areas within close range making it possible for tourists to see a diversity of wildlife within a short period. Tourism circuits can be created to encompass a variety of the country's natural resources. Another asset for the nature tourism industry is that there is already a great deal of national and international promotion of the parks, and Costa Rica is relatively well known as a nature tourism destination.

V. Monteverde Cloud Forest Reserve (Case Study #1)

A. General Description and Infrastructure

Monteverde is a private conservation unit of 10,000 hectares, located between 800 and 1,860 meters above sea level, in the Tilaran Mountains of Northern Costa Rica, 157 kilometers from the capital city of San Jose. The reserve is owned and managed by the Tropical Science Center, a non-profit Costa Rican association. Monteverde is best known for its wealth of wildlife and its lush green forests. It is also the habitat of the endemic golden toad. The presence of these toads, and many other forest dwellers, have made the reserve one of Costa Rica's main tourist attractions.

During the early 1950s, Monteverde was practically virgin land, surrounded by untouched primary forest. Cultivated land ended at the foot of the mountains. With land reform laws that favored agricultural expansion, and a natural growth in population, the agricultural frontier moved up the slopes.

In the late 1950's a small community of North American Quakers, seeking peace and a nonviolent society, came to settle in the peaceful, isolated Costa Rican mountains. The Quakers bought 1,400 hectares, divided it among themselves, and set aside 554 hectares for watershed conservation. The newcomers turned their parcels of forest into pastures and dairy farms. They started a small cheese factory. Business began to thrive, and the factory grew. New settlers came from other regions of Costa Rica looking for land. They founded Santa Elena, and, further down the mountain, San Luis, Canitas, and Cabeceras. They also began to produce milk for sale to the factory. Dairy farming was the foundation of the region's economy and has remained so to this day.

In the 1960s, biologists and students began arriving to study the area. The rich cloud forest, still quite unaltered, was very attractive to these students, most of them U.S. biologists. The Organization for Tropical Studies, an international consortium of universities, often brought groups of students and scientists to the area. The Tropical Science Center, also formed during the 1960s, began to take researchers to Monteverde.

The studies of biologists led to the description of many rare species found in the area and also to the discovery of the golden toad. This species' entire range lies within a few acres of Monteverde's cloud forest.

Interest in preserving a representative sample of this biological wealth began to grow. At the same time, the Quaker

43

settlers were working on expanding the protected watershed area. Bosque Eterno, the Monteverde-based conservationists, and the Tropical Science Center of San Jose-based scientists, discovered they had common goals. In 1972, they reached an agreement and the Monteverde Cloud Forest Reserve was founded.

Scientists came in growing numbers to this misty land, to study the habits of bell-birds or photograph umbrella-birds. Macaws, quetzals, tinamous, agoutis, and kinkajous were common sights. Jaguars and ocelots have been reported. Palms, ferns, mosses, bromeliads, immense oaks, and tiny mushrooms were studied. The accounts of these scientists began to attract more visitors to the reserve. Films, new articles, and more stories increased the number of visitors from 300 in 1973 to nearly 13,000 in 1987.

The reserve grew as well, from an original 2,000 hectares to 10,000 hectares. The new lands have been bought with donations, collected mostly by the Monteverde Conservation League, a local nongovernmental organization formed in 1987. This is a very active local association, working for the conservation of the reserve, environmental education of neighbor communities, and careful regulation of the growing visitation.

B. Visitor Information to Date

Since 1980, Monteverde has become an increasingly popular destination for nature-oriented tourists. As can be seen from Table 5, visitation more than tripled in six years.

Table 5.

VISITOR DAYS TO MONTEVERDE CLOUD FOREST RESERVE
1980 - 1985

YEAR	VISITOR DAYS
1980	3,257
1981	6,498
1982	5,924
1983	6,786
1984	8,985
1985	11,762
TOTAL	43,212

Source: Monteverde Cloud Forest Reserve, 1988

C. WWF Park Survey Results

1. Visitor Profile

Specific data on visitor patterns and profiles were obtained during our two survey weeks,[1] when a total of 84 international visitors and 26 national visitors[2] were interviewed.

Over two-thirds of all visitors were North Americans (74 percent), and another 20 percent were Europeans. A majority of visitors were male (57 percent) with a mean age of 36.9. Visitors tend to arrive at Monteverde by bus (60 percent) or by automobile (39 percent) and are generally accompanied by friends or colleagues (38 percent) or relatives (27 percent). About 15 percent indicated that they came with a tour group. An overwhelming majority had planned their excursion to Monteverde before coming to Costa Rica (90 percent), while the remainder decided to visit the reserve based upon recommendations from friends or relatives, advice from local people, or other sources.

The most commonly listed reasons for visiting Monteverde were its flora (mentioned by 62 percent), fauna (56 percent), rare species (36 percent), adventure (26 percent), and geology (25 percent). Nature-related activities of visitors included birdwatching (74 percent), wildlife observation (67 percent), hiking (55 percent), botany (41 percent), and rain forest excursions (47 percent).

About 16 percent of the visitors indicated that they had spent at least one night within the reserve, while the majority spent at least one night outside the reserve (82 percent) while visiting Monteverde. The mean number of nights spent in or near the reserve was 7.6.

2. Visitor Impressions

An impressive majority of international visitors described their excursion experience as excellent (42 percent) or good (53 percent). Satisfaction with the reserve's lodge facility was equally high (95 percent). Visitors enjoyed the reserve's natural features, the birdwatching, nature trails and flora, but

---

[1]One week in February (high season), and one week in May (low season)

[2]Due to the small number surveyed, results from nationals are not included.

disliked nature trails that were difficult, the lack of
restaurants, the lack of roads/transport to the park, and the
lack of technical information and checklists.

When asked how their visit to the reserve could be improved,
visitors recommended improving guide books, technical
information, and maps; and improving tourist services in general.
Future problems foreseen by visitors were tourism's increased
effect on the wildlife and environment, erosion, and the overuse
of nature trails.

D. Economic Impact of Tourism at Monteverde

An important source of tourist income at Monteverde has been
entrance fees. The entrance fees are higher than at most other,
public parks in Costa Rica (roughly U.S. $2.75 vs. $.65). This
income has covered maintenance costs of the park in the last few
years. Table 6 shows park expenses and entrance fee income for
1983-87. In 1987, 68 percent of total expenses was for
personnel, 13 percent for maintenance, 15 percent for services,
and 4 percent for tax and others.

Table 6.

ANNUAL INCOME AND EXPENSES
MONTEVERDE CLOUD FOREST RESERVE 1983 - 1987

YEAR	EXPENSES (in colones)	INCOME (in colones)
1983	850,000	1,000,000
1984	950,000	1,250,000
1985	1,399,000	1,335,707
1986	1,375,364	2,181,025
1987	2,676,393	2,740,629
TOTAL	7,250,757	8,507,362

Source: Monteverde Rainforest Reserve, 1988

Tourism has also had an enormous economic impact within the
community that surrounds the reserve. Tourism earnings are the
second largest source of income for local residents after dairy
production. Much infrastructure has developed for tourists,
which has consequently increased the number of people employed in
tourist-related activities. Today there are two hotels, two

pensions, a souvenir and crafts store, horse rentals, and the most recent additions, a disco-bar and a cantina.

The four lodging places have a total of 48 rooms, with a daily capacity of 152 guests. Occupancy at all places is highly seasonal. Permanent employment at the accommodation facilities is low. In addition to the owners, who often work at the hotels, the Hotel de Montaña has nine employees, Quetzal has three, Flor Mar has two, and Belmar has three. However, during high tourist season, employment rates grow to 14 at Hotel de Montaña, 6 at Quetzal, five at Flor Mar and nine at Belmar. Salaries in these facilities are higher than the regional average. (Frueh, 1988)

The souvenir and crafts shop is a very profitable enterprise and annual sales recently reached US $50,000. The shop was founded in 1982 by eight women as a cooperative venture. With the increasing numbers of tourists and the demand for souvenirs from the area, the founders established a coop called CASEM (Cooperative de Artesanos de Santa Elena y Monteverde). CASEM now has 70 members, primarily women with a few men. The members of CASEM produce and sell embroidered shirts and dresses, painted shirts and hats, ceramic and wood-carved souvenirs and other items. Sales doubled between 1987 and 1988 (Frueh, 1988).

Tourism has also increased the demand for guides. While some guides come with tour groups from San Jose, many local residents have become independent guides. Two residents make their primary income as nature guides. In addition, a few locals have been hired directly by travel agencies that bring groups to Monteverde.

In terms of indirect economic benefits, local agriculturalists have not had a great increase in demand for their products because of tourism. Aside from local dairy products, which are of very high quality and used widely among tourist facilities, most other agricultural produce is not produced in the area and is brought in from nearby large towns, such as Puntarenas and Canas.

There is currently much debate among Monteverde residents about the economic impact of tourism. While it is clearly a significant and growing source of income for the area, there are some concerns about this impact. Residents want to ensure that tourism remains small-scale and that benefits are not concentrated in too few hands. Residents are also concerned about that increasing recognition of their area is driving up land prices. Escalating real estate costs have put land around Monteverde among the highest costs per hectare in Costa Rica, and these costs are straining agricultural expansion. The tourism boom is thus seen as a mixed blessing.

E. Environmental Impact of Tourism to Monteverde

The greater visitor numbers have caused some noticeable ecological impacts. New trails have been built inside the reserve, some of which are used mainly for tourism, and others for research. On the tourists' trails, erosion is a serious problem. During the rainy season, the tree roots that border the trails are trampled by visitors. Locals report that the habits of the animals have changed and that some can be seen near the tourist trails only after the high season. On the other hand, visitors bring substantial donations to Monteverde. These have been used to buy new lands and help maintain the reserve.

VI. Volcán Poás National Park (Case Study #2)

A. General Description and Infrastructure

Few active volcanoes in the world are so easily accessible and so well equipped to host visitors as the 3,000-meter-high Volcán Poás. To reach Poás, three different routes can be taken from San Jose. All three routes have spectacular views and traverse some of the most fertile lands in the country. This is perhaps what has made Poás one of Costa Rica's most visited parks.

Poás, located 60 kilometers away from San Jose, is a composite basaltic volcano, with active fumaroles and sporadic geyser-like eruptions. The crater is an enormous depression of 15 meters width and 300 meters depth. The volcano has a long history of eruptions. At irregular intervals, it shoots up columns of steam and muddy water, sometimes as high as 200 meters. From the inner cone of the crater, the hot fumaroles can reach temperatures up to 1,000 degrees Celsius.

A short walk from the active crater, along a trail bordered by dwarf plants, lies an extinct crater. Now rimmed with thick vegetation, the crater has become filled by rain and is called the "Laguna Botos."

In 1955, Poás was declared a "national park." Under the existing legislation, it was the Tourism Institute's responsibility to "manage and protect all lands within a two kilometer radius of all volcanic craters in the country." In 1969, with the creation of the National Parks Department, jurisdiction of Poás was transferred to this department. In 1971, an area of 490 hectares was declared "Poás Volcano National Park." The designated park area has grown since then and now includes 5,317 hectares.

Until 10 years ago, the road to Poás was a muddy trail, and many visitors gave up their attempts to see the crater. It was only in 1979 that the road was finally paved, and Poás became a favorite day excursion. The National Parks Service planned to turn Poas into a "model national park," to show that recreation and conservation could be combined and at the same time, benefits could be provided to neighboring populations.

A master plan for the park's management was designed and large investments were made to build trails, a visitor center, picnic areas, and other facilities. In Costa Rica, no other National Park has such developed infrastructure and facilities, and no other park has such high visitation rates.

B. Visitor Information to Date

Visitation to Poás is concentrated on weekends. On a clear Sunday, it is common for the park to receive 3,000 visitors. They come mostly in large groups that rent an excursion bus and bring food, pets, radios, soccer balls and alcohol. High season months for Poás are December, March, July, and August. In winter, most of the visitors are students in organized groups.

The share of international tourists has fluctuated between 18 percent and almost 30 percent between 1981 and 1985. The number of tourists has increased from 10,898 in 1981 to 23,640 in 1986 (National Park Survey).

C. WWF Park Survey Results

1. Visitor Profile

Data on visitor patterns and profiles were obtained during our two survey weeks[3], when 71 international and 29 national tourists[4] were interviewed.

Main countries or regions of origin were North America (65 percent), Europe (14 percent), Colombia (6 percent), and Panama (4 percent). The majority of international visitors (69 percent) were male; visitors had a mean age of 44.2 and had a mean annual income close to U.S. $40,000. Most visitors were accompanied by relatives (41 percent; mean number: 1.7) or friends and colleagues (34 percent). About 15.5 percent came with a tour group.

The main motivation for visiting Poás was its geology (41 percent), recreation (30 percent), the short distance to San Jose (25 percent), and the park's flora (24 percent). Nature-related activities at Poás included hiking (72 percent), birdwatching (33 percent), wildlife observation (21 percent), botany (21 percent), and jungle excursions (10 percent).

In most cases (69 percent), visitors had planned their excursions to Poás before coming to Costa Rica; the remainder (31 percent) included Poás in their itinerary after they arrived as a result of recommendations from friends and family, brochures, or local residents. Visitors reach the park by

---

[3]One week in February (high season), one week in May (low season).

[4]Due to the relatively small number of national visitors, results from nationals surveyed are not included here.

automobile (53 percent) or bus (43 percent). The mean number of nights spent in or near the park was one.

2. Visitor Impressions

The overwhelming majority of international visitors described their visit as excellent (49 percent) or good (46 percent). The park's infrastructure was evaluated as good (46 percent) or, by some (28 percent) as excellent.

Visitors liked the park's natural features, its nature trails, its flora, and the availability of technical information. Many visitors complained about loud radios brought into the park and about the language barrier (i.e., the existing signs are in Spanish only). When asked how their park visit could be improved, visitors suggested improving guide books, maps, and technical information; improving guide services; better maintenance of toilet facilities; and opening a restaurant.

Few visitors seemed to perceive future problems from tourism, though some mentioned possible effects of tourism on wildlife and the environment and the lack of protection of the environment.

D. Economic Impact of Tourism at Poás

Volcán Poás is located 60 kilometers from San Jose. As with many parks that are located close to a large city, the economic impact of tourism to Poás is minimal to surrounding residents. Despite high visitation figures, there is little demand for overnight facilities at Poás. The only overnight facility is a designated camping area which receive few campers.

On the road to Poás, there are a few restaurants and cafes, totalling just over 300 seats. There are three pensions and one souvenir store. Employment generation at the restaurants is about 16 people during the week and double that number on the weekend. On weekends, there are also a number of street vendors, most of them selling strawberries. For the majority of the people involved with these enterprises, tourism revenue is not their primary source of income.

At the park itself, income generation is even less than on the road to the park. A small entrance fee is collected which covers some of the park maintenance costs. There is a small visitors center but there is no other tourism infrastructure, such as a snack bar or souvenir shop, to sell things to visitors. Therefore the money generated at the park is very limited.

E. Environmental Impacts of Tourism to Poás

Park personnel are scarce, and the park's resources are limited. Normally, only three or four rangers are stationed at the park. This means that they are collecting entrance fees, assisting visitors, presenting the daily slide show, maintaining trails, and making sure regulations are followed. Because of the small staff, most of these functions cannot be performed efficiently on weekends. Litter is common along the paths after the hectic weekends.

However, the park's education program is an important tool in increasing the environmental consciousness of visitors. The visitor center is very informative about the resources of the area. The only difficulty is that most of the signs are in Spanish, which means that there is a missed environmental education opportunity among all non-Spanish speakers.

CHAPTER 3

I. Status of Tourism Industry

A. History and Growth

Dominica is the largest of the Windward Islands in the Caribbean. It is unique in the region in terms of its tourism "product" and its consequent market and strategy for tourism development. Unlike most other Caribbean islands, Dominica has few white sand beaches and therefore attracts few beach tourists. However, the island does have many valuable natural resources. Still 60 percent covered with forests, Dominica has beautiful, rugged, and lush mountainous terrain and has earned the nickname "nature island." Recognizing the tourist potential in its unique resources, the Dominican government is actively trying to develop the tourism industry through the promotion of nature tourism.

Tourist arrivals for the past 12 years have been recorded by the Caribbean Tourism Research Center (CTRC). In these statistics, visitors to Dominica have been divided into two groups. "Excursionists" are visitors who stay less than one day, primarily cruise-ship passengers. "Stay-over visitors" are those who stay more than one day. Total visitor arrivals increased from 22,018 in 1976 to 36,400 in 1986, which is a 65 percent increase.[1] There was a distinct decrease in 1979 and 1980 due to widespread and devastating effects of Hurricanes David and Allen.

---

[1]There are some discrepancies among statistics sources concerning Dominican tourism figures; these discrepancies are reflected throughout the text of this section.

Table 1.

TOURIST ARRIVALS IN DOMINICA
1976-1986

	1976	1977	1978	1979	1980	1981	1982	1983	1984	1985	1986
Total visitor arrivals	22,018	23,547	27,944	20,305	24,900		22,900		27,000	28,600	36,400
Stay-over visitors	16,981	18,919	20,111	15,485	14,000	15,213	19,000	19,500	22,200	21,500	24,400
Cruise ship passengers	1,908	7,500	7,635	7,770	7,400	5,806	2,400	5,359	3,200	6,600	11,500
Other excursionists	4,900	3,966	6,767	4,847	3,100		1,500		1,600	500	500

Source: Esmond Devas WTO/CTRC, Statistical Division, CDB, Grersch 1986

According to a 1986 CTRC survey, Dominica's main tourist markets are the Caribbean, United States, Europe, and Canada. Forty-three percent of all tourists came from other Caribbean islands, about half of these from the neighboring French islands of Guadeloupe and Martinique. The United States and Europe each contributed just over 20 percent, 6 percent were Canadian, and the remaining 9 percent were from other countries. (1986 Visitor Expenditure and Motivation Survey, Dominica, CTRC).

The origins of visitors have also been recorded by the Statistical Division in Dominica. Trends of visitors by country can be seen in Table 2.

Table 2.

VISITOR ARRIVALS BY COUNTRY OF USUAL RESIDENCE

COUNTRY OF USUAL RESIDENCE	1978	1979	1980	1981	1982	1983	1984	1985	1986	1987
U.S.A.	3,594	2,212	2,336	2,409	3,767	4,148	4,231	3,999	5,104	4,968
French West Indies	- - -	3,162	3,162	2,814	3,013	4,441	4,796	4,552	5,285	6,165
U.K.	3,253	1,377	1,464	625	1,922	1,755	1,976	1,789	2,346	2,824
Canada	2,878	788	827	781	982	1,094	1,257	1,130	1,540	1,541
O.E.C.S. countries	5,082	1,567	1,628	1,738	2,119	2,339	2,680	2,988	2,930	3,292
Other CARICOM countries	3,090	1,760	1,568	1,715	2,217	2,352	2,620	2,539	2,637	2,585
Rest of Americas	95	2,546	1,752	2,206	2,482	1,965	2,246	2,325	1,971	2,770
France	- - -	3,652	2,227	887	1,581	2,293	1,579	922	526	817
Other Europe	- - -	3,035	2,240	4,006	1,908	1,738	1,972	1,359	2,287	2,843
Other countries	9,952	59	104	158	159	224	419	359	252	349
Not stated	- - -	147	97	99	256	1	50	- - -	- - -	- - -
Total	27,944	20,305	17,405	17,438	20,406	22,350	23,826	21,962	24,878	28,154

Source: Quarterly Bulletin of Tourism Statistics, prepared and published by the Statistical Division

The Tourism Statistical Division in Dominica has devised a table (Table 3) to show numbers of visitors by purpose of visit. It is interesting to note the large numbers of business travelers as well as "private visitors" who stay with friends and family.

Table 3.

VISITOR ARRIVALS BY PURPOSE OF VISIT

PURPOSE OF VISIT	1979	1980	1981	1982	1983	1984	1985	1986	1987
Hotel visitor	5,297	7,258	7,058	8,523	8,068	9,287	7,213	6,125	6,567
Private visitor	6,667	2,985	3,857	4,897	5,546	6,798	9,035	12,675	14,250
Business visitor	2,589	4,009	3,617	5,350	5,808	6,084	5,084	5,443	160
Excursionists	4,720	3,085	2,297	1,463	2,693	1,619	509	446	1,441
Students	8	1	79	114	200	- -	65	103	5,629
Other	1	7	4	- -	4	- -	16	64	107
Not stated	1,023	60	526	59	31	38	40	- -	- -
Total	20,305	17,405	17,438	20,406	22,350	23,826	21,962	24,856	28,154

Source: Quarterly Bulletin of Tourism Statistics, prepared and published by the Statistical Division

There are few statistics on the foreign exchange earnings from tourism. Recent calculations show that tourism's contribution to Dominica's gross national product was 25.6 percent, or just over U.S. $10 million for 1986 (CTRC, 1986). Income from cruise ship tourism has steadily increased over the years, from U.S. $80,000 in 1977 to U.S. $190,000 in 1986, and will undoubtedly continue to grow.

The government receives both direct and indirect revenue from tourism. Direct sources include: hotel occupancy taxes, embarkation taxes, landing charges, port dues, liquor and entertainment taxes, work permits, and stamp sales. Indirect sources include: import duties on tourism-related goods, income taxes on tourism-related employment, and profit taxes on tourism enterprises.

While firm figures are not available for all of these revenue sources, the Dominica Income Tax Division did calculate the value added of the hotel and restaurant sectors to the GDP for the last six years. These are shown in Table 4.

Table 4.

_____

GOVERNMENT RECEIPTS FROM HOTEL OCCUPANCY AND BAR SALES

	1982	1983	1984	1985	1986	1987
All hotels	124,095	186,576	198,576	197,410	221,617	245,060

_____

Source: Reference Income Tax Division, Dominica, as cited by
Edwards, 1988

_____

A visitor expenditure survey was conducted in 1982 to
determine how visitor revenue contributed to each sector involved
with tourism. The results of the survey can be seen in Table 5.

Table 5.

_____

VISITOR EXPENDITURE BY CATEGORY
(U.S.$m)

CATEGORY	U.S.$m
Accommodations	1.56
Excursionists	.10
Food and beverage	2.15
Others	.56
Total	4.37

_____

Source: Visitor Expenditure Survey - Dominica CTRC, 1982; Luther
Gordon, Miller, February 1984, as cited by Edwards, 1988

_____

Visitor expenditures have also been estimated by other sources.
Grersch (1986) estimates that visitor expenditures increased from

U.S. $2.9 million in 1980, to $4.6 million in 1982, to $5.9 million in 1984, and to $7.1 million in 1986.

The Caribbean Tourism Research Center has estimated the breakdown of expenditures by category of visitor. Again, there are discrepancies in the tourism statistics among these sources.

Table 6.

ESTIMATED TOTAL VISITOR EXPENDITURE BY CATEGORY
(U.S.$m)

ITEM	1977	1978	1979	1980	1981	1982
Business visitors	0.81	1.05	0.52	0.67	0.98	0.51
Vacationers	0.72	0.59	0.72	0.88	1.10	1.20
Visitors, friends and relatives	0.34	0.41	0.82	0.33	0.65	0.79
Day visitors	0.10	0.20	0.17	0.10	0.09	0 .66
Cruise ship passengers	0.08	0.08	0.09	0.08	0.09	0.04
Total	2.05	2.33	2.32	2.06	2.91	3.60

Source: Tourism development Strategy, CDB - 1980; WTO/CTRC, 1980; CTRC, 1986, as cited by Edwards, 1988

Employment generation related to tourism has been minimal thus far in Dominica. In 1978, it was estimated that about 250 persons were employed in tourist accommodation facilities, including staff employed to lead tours. An additional 250 persons were estimated to be employed indirectly through tourism, specifically in transportation and services (Edwards, 1988).

A recent estimate shows that in 1987, at least 1,000 jobs were created in tourism-related businesses, including hotels, restaurants, entertainment, handicrafts and taxis. (Greish, EEC Tourism Advisor, 1987).

B. Major Tourism Attractions

Most of the tourism attractions in Dominica are natural areas. The island has two national parks, Morne Trois Pitons and Cabrits, and two forest reserves, Northern and Central. These large protected areas have several important smaller areas within their borders.

Another major attraction is the Carib Indian Reservation which is located in the northeastern part of the island. The Carib Indians were the first inhabitants of Dominica. They live on the reservation, where they maintain their own Carib chief. Currently, there are many visitors to the reservation (no statistics available). There are few specific tourist attractions on the reserve to date, except for a few small gift shops with excellent Carib handicrafts, including baskets, placemats, etc. However, a negative environmental impact is that the plant materials to make these crafts are decreasing. The natives are also planning to develop other means to demonstrate their lifestyle to visitors.

C. Tourism Policy, Management, and Promotion

The Ministry of Tourism and the Tourism Board are the administrative agencies in charge of the development and promotion of tourism. The Ministry of Tourism controls and directs tourism and produces guidelines on policies and strategies. The Tourism Board is a statutory body financed by the Ministry of Tourism; it advises the Ministry and implements its tourism policies.

The Board consists of a director, support staff, and appointed members from private and public sector organizations that have a direct relation to the tourist trade. The Board recently merged with the Industrial Development Corporation, the agency that promotes investment in the country. The two organizations form the National Development Corporation.

The government has taken legal steps to encourage tourism development. Under the Hotel Aids Ordinance Act, all articles of hotel equipment and building material for hotel construction is free from import duty. In addition, all shareholders of a hotel are exempted from income tax on dividends distributed during the first 12 years of operation.

A tourism policy was recently developed. In very broad terms, the government committed itself to provide the basic conditions necessary for lasting tourism growth so as to optimize the sector's contribution to the national economy in terms of net value added. The development of tourism is to be based on the full participation of the people of Dominica and is to be developed in order to improve the quality of life in Dominica, create employment and foreign exchange, and enhance and preserve the cultural and natural resources of the country.

The government wants to attract tourists who like what Dominica already has (Okey, 1987). Dominicans do not want to become another "Caribbean beach resort," but want to target their tourism market to visitors who come to enjoy undisturbed natural resources. Dominicans are promoting their country as the "Nature Island of the Caribbean."

The government has recently stated its intentions to improve the tourism infrastructure. Improvements thus far include resurfacing over 18.6 miles (30 km) of roads, the renovation of the Canefield airstrip in Roseau, a new terminal at Canefield, and a feasibility study for a new airport. It has also been observed that in addition to more space at the airport, the airline service is better. A three-year program was launched in 1988 to upgrade tourism facilities. Twelve natural area tourism sites have been chosen. Picnic and restroom areas as well as directional signs will be improved or developed in these areas to encourage more visitors.

II. Status of Tourism to Protected Areas

A. Demand for Tourism to Protected Areas

No statistics have been collected at any protected site in Dominica to record the number or origin of visitors. However, given that the majority of tourist attractions on Dominica are nature-oriented, any overall increase in tourism can safely be said to reflect an increasing interest in the country's natural areas. In addition, through conversations with people involved with tourism near protected areas, including lodge owners and nature guides, it is evident that the numbers of nature tourists are growing.

Tourists who visit Dominica tend to stay in the capital, Roseau and take day trips to various natural attractions. Prior to the present study, the only statistical indication of the importance of Dominica's natural areas for visitors is the Visitor Expenditure and Motivation Survey (CTRC, winter and summer of 1986). Among the list of motives for coming to Dominica, over 90 percent of those surveyed marked "tropical setting." This term, however, encompasses many different activities.

There is increasing interest in Dominica as a SCUBA diving destination. A second dive shop has opened, which reflects this growing interest. Also, a recent issue of Skin Diver Magazine featured an article on diving in Dominica.

Surveys were conducted during this study at the Canefield airport to determine the degree to which natural protected areas influenced tourists' travel plans and activities. After the collection of socio-demographic information, visitors were asked how important protected areas were in their decision to visit the country, how many protected areas they visited, and what kinds of nature-oriented activities they participated in during their trip.

WWF Airport Survey Results

Socio-demographic Information

Average age: 37.9 years, youngest 16, oldest 90 years
                      old (N=62).

Average nights:	Average number of nights was 14.5; shortest stay was overnight, longest was 70 (N=75).
Family members:	Of the 83 tourists surveyed, 28 (34 percent) came with family members. Average was between three and four total family members. The largest family group had six people.
Expenditures:	Seventy-one of the 83 people surveyed reported an average total expenditure of $,1429, with $211 being the average daily expenditure (N=66). The highest cost vacation was more than $9,999, and the cheapest vacation cost $75. Of the 83 respondents, 35 people reported an average expenditure of $844 for airfare.
Income:	The average family income was between $20,000 and $30,000, although most people surveyed reported incomes over $30,000.
Gender:	53 percent of respondents were men, 47 percent were women.
Nationality:	The nationality distribution of the survey respondents (N=83) was as follows: 33.7 percent North American, 30.1 percent European, 21.7 percent Guyanese, 6 percent Dominican, and 8.4 percent all other.

Protected Areas and Nature-oriented Tourism

Although Dominica's nickname is "The Nature Island," tourism that results strictly from a desire to enjoy the parks and protected areas is still relatively small-scale. However, this may indicate a great deal of growth potential to specifically target and promote certain types of outdoor activities. In the survey, respondents gave their reasons for visiting in terms of how important natural areas were in their decisions to travel to Dominica. The reponses follow:

Main reason	13%
Important, influenced decision	12%
Somewhat important	25%
Not important	35%
No response	15%

The majority (61 percent) of people visiting Dominica had been there before, while 39 percent were first-time visitors to the island. The top five reasons given for visiting were:

Visit friends or family	58%
Sun/beaches/recreation	28%
Business	27%
Sightseeing	23%
Natural history	21%

Once in Dominica, the activities most commonly enjoyed by all tourists were nature-based. Although tourists gave multiple responses, it is important that a very high percentage, no matter what their reason for travel to the country, participated in nature-based activities:

Local cultures	25%
Hiking/trekking	18%
Mountaineering	17%
Jungle excursions	16%
Wildlife observing	15%
Birdwatching	13%
Botany	12%
Boat trips	8%
Hunting/fishing	2%

Visitors surveyed were asked to list what they most liked and disliked about their stay in Dominica. The "friendliness of the people" was listed most frequently, by 39 of 83 visitors surveyed, as what they liked most. Dominica's "natural resources, natural features and beauty" was recorded by 28 visitors, and the country's "local festival" was highlighted in 13 surveys. Of the 83 visitors surveyed, 14 commented on the country's "airport facilities and services" as what they disliked most about their visit. Another dislike, listed by 8 visitors, was the "road system, and lack of road signs."

B. Supply of Protected Areas

As mentioned earlier in the report, there are four main protected areas in Dominica that contain several natural areas within their boundaries.

Morne Trois Pitons National Park

This national park was created as a result of the National Park and Protected Areas Act (1975). The 17,000-acre (6883 ha) park is located in the south central interior of the island. The objectives for establishing the park were to protect the natural resources and ecology of the area; to provide the local people with a natural setting for recreational purposes; to serve as a natural laboratory for education and research; and to stimulate industries capable of boosting the island's economy, specifically the tourism industry.

The park encompasses four mountain peaks, the Morne Trois Pitons (4,537 ft/1,383 m), Morne Macaque (3,674 ft/1,120 m), Morne Watt (3,953 ft/1,205 m), and Morne Anglais (3,996 ft/ 1,218 m). Water resources play an important role in the park and are a big tourist attraction. In addition to numerous rivers and streams, the park contains several waterfalls. The two largest inland basins on Dominica are located in the park. These crater lakes, the Freshwater Lake (2,500 ft) and the Boeri Lake (2,800 ft) were formed between the volcanic dome of the Morne Micotrin and its partially buried crater.

One of the biggest attractions of Morne Trois Pitons is its rich tropical vegetation. Untouched Caribbean forest can be found within four types of vegetation zones. The high altitudes provide wet, windy climates ideal for ferns, mosses, and lichens that create a low ground cover vegetation known as Elfin Woodland or Cloud Forest. Rain forests make up the lower levels, with a rich vegetation comprising a complex variety of trees, vines, shrubs, and undergrowth. The rivers and coastal areas of the park are still other sources for vegetation types, allowing for a widely varying range of plant and bird life.

From Roseau, there are three major access routes to the park: Laudat, Trafalgar Falls (one of the case studies in this report), and Wotten Waven. During the 1970s, a system of trails and picnic areas was developed within the park, but the 1979 hurricane destroyed the infrastructure. At present, 12 sites within the park are being upgraded.

One of the most visited sites within the park is Emerald Pool. Located at the northernmost tip of the park, its main attractions are a large tract of rain forest, a waterfall, and a large pool. Many Dominicans frequent the pool on weekends to bathe.

Two other significant areas in the park are the Boiling Lake and the Valley of Desolation. The Boiling Lake is the second largest in the world and is located at 2,500 feet (762 m.) The Valley of Desolation lies adjacent to the lake and contains numerous fumeroles. Because of the hot sulfur fumes from the lake, the valley has a distinct vegetation. Currently, access to both these areas is extremely difficult. One must travel by rough trail, with a guide, for approximately three hours each way. Therefore, few people make the trek each year. There are discussions now in Dominica about developing an infrastructure to facilitate accessibility to Boiling Lake and the Valley of Desolation.

It has been difficult to maintain Morne Trois Pitons for a variety of reasons. The Forestry and Parks Service, under whose aegis the park falls, does not have an budget for overall maintenance. Also, the topography makes maintenance difficult. The vegetation grows very rapidly and thus constant trail maintenance is required. The high rainfall in the areas also takes a toll on the trails.

Cabrits Historical and National Park

This park was recently established through an Act of Parliament in 1987. It is located approximately a mile (1.6 km) north from Dominica's second largest city, Portsmouth, and about 20 miles (32.3 km) from Roseau. The original park concept included Cabrits Historical Monument and Marine Park. However, to date, the National Park Act has not been amended to make allowances for the protection of marine areas within Dominica's territorial waters.

The park consists of four major zones: a) Cabrits Peninsula; b) the swamps, containing important nesting areas for local and migratory birds; c) the beach front; and d) the marine areas and associated coral community. All four components provide unique features important for historical, recreational, and scientific purposes. Two vegetation types are represented within this area. The hills are covered by a dry scrub forest, a result of the relatively low precipitation. The adjoining lands are wetlands, which consist mainly of a marsh that is inundated for several months each year.

The park is accessible by trail or by road up to 40 feet (12.2 m) from the gate. The access road is being repaired at present. There is a small museum at the park and the area is becoming a focal point for both national and international tourism and historical education.

Forest Reserves

There are two forest reserves, both in the north central part of the island. The Central Forest Reserve contains 1,103 acres (410 ha), and the Northern Forest Reserve 21,771 acres (8,814 ha). The Northern Forest Reserve provides habitat to two endemic and endangered parrot species, the Sisserou and Red-necked Parrots, which are major tourist attractions. Recently, threats to the parrots' habitat have resulted from uncontrolled logging as well as the conversion of some land for agriculture use. Controlled logging is permitted in the reserve.

III. Impacts of Tourism to Protected Areas

A. Economic Activities Related to Nature Tourism

It is difficult to calculate the exact contribution of economic activities related to nature tourism. However, indicators of economic activities related to nature tourism in Dominica can be seen in trends among tour operators and in the kinds of services they offer. Information about economic impacts can also be ascertained by analyzing the job opportunities emerging from tourist demand at specific sites.

Dominica has seven local tour operators. They are Dominica Tours, Rainbow Rovers, Emerald Safari Tours, Wilderness Tours, Whitechurch Travel Agency, Tony Burnette Biscombe, and Mally Reltier. All seven agencies offer nature tours and are finding increasing demand for this type of tourism. Much of the demand is for taxi service to visit the natural areas.

Another way to analyze economic impact is to look at individual sites. At Trafalgar Falls, there is a guest house at the base of the falls called Papillote. In addition to providing accommodations, Papillote offers a restaurant and a craft shop. Several village residents work at the guest house as well as make handicrafts for the gift shop. The owner of the guest house claims that her business has a sizable impact on the local community. She pays over U.S. $22,000 in salaries to her staff per year. To retain tour operators for her guests, she pays almost U.S. $200 per week, and for local produce she pays U.S. $150 per week.

Trafalgar Falls has no permanent park staff. The Forestry Department is in charge of park maintenance, but no one is stationed onsite on a daily basis.

Less economic activity surrounds Emerald Pool because there are no facilities in the park where people can spend money. The Emerald Pool Guest House is located close to the park; however, its occupancy rate is very low, partly due to its lack of telephone service. The owner of the guest house also indicated that it was problematic to recruit people to work in the guest house because it is not in the capital city where people prefer to work.

An interesting tourism debate in Dominica is the economic benefits vs. the environmental and social costs imposed by cruise ship passengers. The number of cruise ship passengers has increased from 770 in 1979 to 12,080 in 1987. (Central Statistical Office, 1988). It is argued by some that this increase is a good source of revenue for Dominica, especially for some tour operators. Others argue that cruise ship passengers actually spend very little on the island because they do not stay overnight and since all their meals are furnished on the ship, they also spend little on food and beverage.

At the same time, cruise ship passengers arrive in great numbers and can have an overwhelming impact on natural areas that are not set up to receive so many visitors. Further, they are generally not the type of "nature tourist" that the island is trying to attract. There is discussion of developing a harbor commercial area to "contain" cruise ship passengers. For the present, the question of how to balance the positive and negative impacts of these tourists is a challenging one.

B. Positive and Negative Environmental Impacts

1. Conservation Activities and Environmental Education

RARE Center for Tropical Bird Conservation and ICBP are currently working with the Dominican government to protect an area of prime parrot habitat. An education campaign is now underway, and an informational visitor center is also planned.

2. Negative Environmental Impacts

No thorough scientific studies on the negative impacts of tourism have been completed to date. However, through discussions with park personnel, tour operators, and local residents, the following negative impacts have been informally documented. In many of the natural areas, there is a litter problem, often due to the lack of garbage disposal facilities. Cruise ships also dump garbage that invariably sweeps ashore and pollutes beach areas. This has caused widespread concern among the local population who use these areas for recreation and fishing.

Another environmental problem is the use of soap in rivers and natural pools. It has also been observed that flowers and other plants are often collected in protected areas. While the National Parks Act theoretically provides protection against such activity, a lack of personnel prevents monitoring on a daily basis.

Many people involved with the nature tourism industry point to cruise ship passengers as the biggest offenders in these environmental problems. Because cruise ship passengers are generally not nature-oriented tourists and because they come in such large numbers at one time, their overall impact is usually more destructive than that of other tourists who visit natural areas.

C. Sociocultural Considerations

While sociocultural issues were not a focus of this study, it is essential that such considerations be a component of nature tourism development. Many Dominicans expressed the importance of keeping their culture intact as tourism expands. They do not want to become another Caribbean island that is completely dependent on tourism. Therefore, great efforts will be made on the island to ensure that local customs and traditions are maintained as tourism increases.

IV. Obstacles and Opportunities for Growth of Nature Tourism

A. Obstacles for Growth

In Dominica, there are four major obstacles to growth of the nature tourism industry. The first is inadequate funding for park maintenance. Secondly, there is a lack of tourism infrastructure in the park; thirdly, there is a lack of trained guides to give nature tours; and finally, international promotion is lacking for tourism to Dominica.

B. Opportunities for Growth

Dominica has many factors in its favor as it develops its nature tourism industry. Its environment is very rich and virtually intact. Dominica also has many citizens who are interested in promoting nature tourism and some seeking to make investments or find investors for tourism infrastructure.

V. Emerald Pool (Case Study #1)

A. General Description and Infrastructure

Emerald Pool is located at the northern-most tip of the Morne Trois Pitons National Park. The most accessible point in Morne Trois Pitons National Park, Emerald Pool can be reached from the main road along a short trail. It is about 5 acres (2.02 ha) in size. The area's attractions are the waterfall, with a pool at its base, and large tracts of rain forest. Emerald Pool was the first component of the national park that received basic tourism infrastructure.

The park[2] has a well-developed trail system and several lookout points. However, it lacks interpretive signs, a visitor center, and monitoring and control of visitor arrivals. The park has a designated exit and entrance, yet no facilities or manpower for assessing visitors. One brochure is available that describes the area and identifies the flora and the bird life found within the park. Emerald Pool is about 8 miles (13 km) from the nearest community, the Castle Bruce Community. However, there is a guest house within 1 mile (1.6 km)--the Emerald Pool Guest House.

Emerald Pool is managed by the Forestry and Park Service but apart from general administration, the park receives only sporadic care from park personnel. There is no specific budget for Emerald Pool, and it is maintained under the general park maintenance budget.

Prior to Hurricane David in 1979, there were picnic tables, toilet facilities, and a forest ranger assigned to the park for distribution of information material to visitors. To date, this service has not been restored, although construction is planned to place trails, picnic facilities, and directional signs.

B. Visitor Information to Date

No mechanism has been put into place to monitor visitation to the park. However, Emerald Pool is commonly cited as one of the focal areas of visitation of the Dominican park system. All cruise ship visitors visit the area during the cruise ship season, which lasts from October to April. Most visitors engage in sightseeing, photography, and swimming. Some are interested in the botanical species of the area. However, without a

---

[2]Emerald Pool is called a "park" throughout this report although it is only a small fraction of Morne Trois Pitons National Park.

regular guide service, most visitors do not have a means to learn about the resources of the area.

C. WWF Park Survey Results

1. Visitor Profile

Data on visitor patterns and profiles were obtained during two survey weeks,[3] when 83 international visitors were interviewed.

Over 81 percent of all international visitors came from North America, and another 16 percent came from Europe. The majority of visitors were male (60 percent); their average age was 47, and their mean annual incomes between U.S. $30,000 and $39,999.

The vast majority of visitors were accompanied by relatives (91 percent). A smaller percentage (24 percent) were accompanied by friends and colleagues or a tour group (14 percent). The main means of transportation used to get to the Park were automobile (38 percent), bus (38 percent), or boat (16 percent).

The main reasons cited for visiting Emerald Pool were its flora (24 percent), the short distance from Roseau (19 percent), its geology (17 percent), and adventure (16 percent). Nature-related activities included hiking, jungle excursion, botany, and wildlife observation.

2. Visitor Impressions

Visitors' impressions of Emerald Pool as a tourist destination were obtained from the WWF park survey. All visitors described their visit to the park as either excellent (55 percent) or good (45 percent). Eighty-eight percent were satisfied with the park's infrastructure, while 10 percent described the infrastructure as mediocre.

Visitors enjoyed the park's natural features and resources, its flora, the guides, and the waterfalls. Some visitors disliked the difficulty of the nature trails, and the lack of interpretive and technical information.

Asked for suggestions on how to improve the park, visitors recommended improving maps, technical information, and

---

[3]One week in February (high season), and one week in May (low season).

guidebooks on the area as well as improving the quality of nature trails.

Some visitors expressed concerns about increased future tourism effects on the wildlife and environment, and saw potential problems with the hazardous nature trail and overlooks.

D. Economic Impact

Cruise ship tour operators benefit to a considerable extent from tourism to Dominica. In addition to this, taxi drivers take visitors on tours to Emerald Pool at a rate of U.S. $15 an hour for an average duration of three hours. Other tourists rent cars to go to the park at rates of U.S. $20-40 per day.

The Emerald Pool Guest House located close to the park provides accommodation for people who wish to stay overnight, but, as mentioned previously, the lack of telephone service and the difficulty of recruiting local people as employees keep the occupancy rate very low. Two local business people have indicated interest in constructing hotels near the park, because of the park's potential importance for international tourism.

E. Environmental Impact

There are no obvious environmental impacts from tourism, except for litter left behind by visitors, mainly due to the fact that there are inadequate garbage disposal facilities. There have been some complaints about the use of detergent soap in the pool.

A common complaint concerning visual pollution has been that some visitors inscribe their names on the rocks surrounding the pool.

VI. Trafalgar Falls (Case Study #2)

A. General Description and Infrastructure

Trafalgar Falls is a privately protected area 5 miles (8.1 km) from Roseau and is located at an elevation of 1,200 feet (366 m). The area has a mean temperature of 72 degrees Fahrenheit and gets about 250 inches (6.4 m) of rain annually. Trafalgar Falls consists of two large waterfalls flowing into the Roseau River Valley. The height of the falls is approximately 150 feet (46 m), and during heavy rains, a third very narrow fall is noticeable. The falls are surrounded by lush tropical vegetation, mainly secondary forest.

The Falls are not part of the Dominican Park System, but they receive a certain amount of protection and attention from the government, and the area is officially managed by the Forestry Division. Once again there is no specific budget for the area, and funds come from the general park maintenance budget. All maintenance to the area is done by the Forestry Division and to a certain extent by the Dominica Electricity Services, which has a power plant close to the falls and utilizes some of the water for hydroelectric purposes.

At present there is an unpaved road leading up to a short trail to the falls. The trail is maintained as well by the Forestry Division and leads through secondary rain forest to a viewing platform. From there, one can view the twin waterfalls. Many visitors take a bath in the pool and cascades formed by the falls.

Trafalgar Falls has no permanent staff. Apart from the general administrative personnel at the Forestry Division, no staff is allocated to the park. No informational material is available on the falls to visitors who go there, nor are there interpretive signs in the park.

B. Visitor Information to Date

The park's visitation patterns are very similar to those of the Emerald Pool.[4] All cruise ship visitors who go on tours are brought to Trafalgar Falls as one of the island's most important natural attractions. Trafalgar Falls is more popular than Emerald Pool since it is close to Roseau and has a restaurant and

---

[4]The Trafalgar Falls Park Survey results were unrepresentative and deemed as not being a random sample since only 13 people responded to the survey during one week in high season (February).

guesthouse nearby. Tourists engage in sightseeing, photography, and river bathing.

C. WWF Park Survey Results

The WWF study intended to include survey information from this park, however difficulty in interviewing people at this location precluded the collection of sufficient representative data.

D. Economic Impact

The main economic impact of tourism to Trafalgar Falls is felt at the guesthouse, managed by an American/Dominican couple. The guesthouse provides accommodations for guests and incorporates a restaurant and a craft shop. Several village residents are employeed in the restaurant and guest house, and tour guides who live in the village are retained to take visitors on tours. The owner of the guest house claims that her business alone has a sizable economic impact on the local community.

E. Environmental Impact

Large numbers of cruise ship visitors visit the Trafalgar Falls area and, although there has been concern about the impact, particularly erosion, there has been no evidence thus far to justify this fear. The owner of the restaurant, also maintains a private botanical garden, has noted that some visitors steal plants and flowers.

CHAPTER 4

ECUADOR

I. Status of Tourism Industry

A. History and Growth

Until the late 1960s, the tourism industry in Ecuador was very small and limited to a few adventure travelers from North America and Europe, as well as some border tourism from Colombia and Peru. In 1969, the cruise ship "Lina A" began to offer tours to the Galapagos Islands, and a new tourist boom began.

International and national tour operators such as Ecuadorian Tours, Metropolitan Touring, and Turismundial all began to focus on trips to the islands. Tourist arrivals to Ecuador increased over 200 percent between 1973 (117,684 visitors) and 1980 (244,485 visitors), with the Galapagos as the primary tourist attraction.

In the 1980's tourism in Ecuador has been variable overall. It continued to expand in 1981 (271,171), then declined for the next three years--with 231,909 in 1982, 197,200 in 1983, and 203,644 in 1984--and then began another upward swing to 233,652 in 1985 and reaching 266,761 in 1986. (General Directorate of Civil Aviation, 1988).

The two principal sources for figures on tourist arrivals are the National Tourism Board, DITURIS, and the National Statistics Institute, INEC. Both extract their data from the arrival forms collected by the immigration department. Although the two groups vary sometimes in their statistics, the trends are uniform: the main sources of tourists are Colombia, North America, and Europe, in particular West Germany and Spain. Arrivals from Europe have been declining in recent years. Arrivals from North America have fluctuated, often as a result of economic conditions (The Economist, 1987).

Despite the rises and falls in numbers of tourist arrivals, tourism has maintained a significant position in the Ecuadorean economy over the last 15 years. It has become the second most important earner of foreign exchange after petroleum products. In 1985, tourism brought about U.S. $260 million to the economy (The Economist, 1987).

For 1982, DITURIS estimates that trip expenditures for foreign arrivals by air were slightly over U.S. $900 for an average length of stay of 17.3 days. During this same period, overland arrivals (mostly from Colombia and Peru) spent an

77

average of U.S. $260 in Ecuador, with an average length of stay of 20.6 days (DITURIS, 1982). Consequently, average daily expenditures for foreign arrivals by air were approximately U.S. $52 and for terrestrial arrivals, U.S. $12.

The National Institute of Statistics and Census estimate that about 2.4 percent of the Ecuadorean labor force was directly employed in the tourism industry in 1986. A total of 4,919 tourist service establishments (hotels, restaurants, bars, and discotheques only) employed 10,979 people.

B. Major Tourism Attractions

Tourism in Ecuador combines culture and folklore with nature and adventure. In addition to the Galapagos, another important tourist attraction is Quito, the capital. Like the Galapagos, Quito is a UNESCO World Heritage Site. Tours in Quito take visitors to colonial churches and monasteries, museums, and galleries, and to a site not far from the city that marks the equator. At least ten small and medium-sized cities of the Andean highlands feature Indian markets. The most popular craft items include Indian weaving, Panama hats, silver jewelry, wood carvings, and leather goods.

In addition to Quito, there is also significant tourism activity along the Pacific coast, which offers deep sea fishing and a limited amount of beach tourism.

In 1982, DITURIS coordinated an inventory of tourism attractions in Ecuador. The inventory was funded by the United Nations Development Programme (UNDP). Including the mountains, lakes, beaches, natural reserves, archaeological ruins, native people resources, and major cities, UNDP identified 877 tourism attractions. These attractions included 510 natural sites, 136 folklore events, 130 cultural events, 57 programmed events, and 44 technical, scientific, or artistic achievements. This inventory is currently being updated (The Economist, 1987).

C. Tourism Policy, Management, and Promotion

Although it was the private sector that gave tourism its first big push in the late 1960s, the government formed the National Tourism Board in 1974 to develop the tourism industry. At the same time, the government also passed the Tourism Development law to regulate activities in the tourism sector (travel agencies and hotels, for example) and to provide incentives for investment in tourism.

Under the administration of the Ministry of Industry, Commerce and Integration, the role of DITURIS is to coordinate the tourism industry, specifically integrating the public and private sectors. DITURIS has three main departments--promotion, technical operations, and administration. The functions of these departments include: regulating restaurant and hotel prices, approving licenses for tourism enterprises and for duty-free imports of capital equipment for tourism businesses, evaluating tourism projects and providing technical assistance, gathering and disseminating statistical information, preparing and distributing promotional material, working with international and domestic airlines to promote tourism to and within Ecuador, training, and encouraging private investment for tourism projects as needed (Coe and Gee, 1986).

In 1984, a Master Development Program for Tourism was drafted. The plan outlined priorities for tourism development as well as constraints. Among the priorities identified were the development of beaches in each of the coastal provinces, the provision of basic services--drinking water, sewers, electric light--and the improvement of statistics and tourist information, such as handbooks. The primary constraint listed was inadequate promotion and lack of high-quality accommodations (The Economist, 1987).

By 1987, however, the supply of hotel rooms remained limited. That year 1,077 hotels with 23,531 hotel rooms were registered with DITURIS. But the majority were of second- or third-class category, with only a small percentage of five-star or first-class hotels (Frueh, 1988).

II. Status of Tourism to Protected Areas

A. Demand for Tourism to Protected Areas

Although statistics have not been consistently kept at all protected areas in Ecuador, parks where they have been recorded generally show upward trends in visitation. For example, at Galapagos, tourism has risen from 17,123 in 1982 to 32,595 in 1987. (The 1987 figure is the official government figure, but other estimates put the visitation level at 49,000). Pasochoa Protection Forest, which is owned by the state and managed under contract by Fundacion Natura, is located outside of Quito. This protected area received 8,107 visitors in 1986 and 17,749 in 1987 (Fundacion Natura, pers. comm.). Limoncocha Biological Reserve had 1,835 visitors in 1986 and 2,676 in 1987 (Metropolitan Touring). Cotopaxi National Park has seen a decrease in visitation from 51,228 visitors in 1982 to 33,196 in 1987.

Table 1.

COTOPAXI NATIONAL PARK
NATIONAL AND INTERNATIONAL VISITORS
1977 - 1987

YEAR	NATIONALS	%	INTERNATIONALS	%	TOTAL
1977	23,044	90.7	2,375	9.3	25,419
1978	25,345	87.7	3,574	12.4	28,919
1979	36,487	85.7	6,114	14.4	42,600
1980	39,504	88.4	5,208	11.6	44,712
1981	n.a.	n.a.	n.a.	n.a.	49,743
1982	n.a.	n.a.	n.a.	n.a.	51,158
1983	n.a.	n.a.	n.a.	n.a.	46,248
1984	n.a	n.a.	n.a.	n.a.	43,453
1985	n.a.	n.a.	n.a.	n.a.	47,279
1986	n.a.	n.a.	n.a.	n.a.	41,316
1987	28,166	84.8	5,030	15.2	33,196

Source: Visitor Registration, Cotopaxi National Park, 1988

80

Table 2.

VISITOR REGISTRATION FOR ECUADOR'S NATURAL AREAS

Natural Areas/(Creation)	1977	1978	1979	1980	1981	1982	1983	1984	1985	1986	1987	1988
Cotopaxi National Park (Aug-75)	25,419	28,919	42,600	44,661	49,743	51,158	46,248	43,453	47,279	41,316	33,196	15,750
Galapagos National Park (May-36)	7,788	12,299	11,692	17,539	16,323	17,124	17,766	18,859	17,850	26,023	33,196	18,880
Machalilla National Park (July-79)	---	---	---	517	820	1,420	2,530	2,250	8,897		2,983	4,097
Podocarpus National Park (Dec-82)	---	---	---	---	---	---	52	80	150	133	175	103
Sangay National Park (June-75)					483	776	945	1,796	652		1,438	336
Limoncocha Biol. Res. (Sept- 85)	---	---	---	---	---	---	---		3,127	2,974	2,676	
Cayambe-Coca Ecological Reserve (Nov-70)				1,512	3,520	10,112	9,715	6,398	2,450		9,056	1,053
Cotacachi-Cayapas Ecological Reserve (Aug-68)					5,235	17,629	29,116	53,185	84,398		95,077	45,539
Pululahua Geobotanical Reserve (Jan-66)						1,188	2,773	4,036	5,325	3,245	3,380	1,401
Cuyabeno Wildlife Production Reserve (July-79)	---	---	---			40	12	141	155	365	185	60
Boliche Recreation Area (July-79)	---	---	---	35,063	43,416	43,904	43,416	40,181	34,869		40,932	17,164
Cajas Recreation Area (June-77)	---	16,000	16,640	17,000	19,200	22,400	25,100	32,000	40,240	48,000	53,800	

Source: M.A.G. - Direccion Nacional Forestal

WWF's airport survey at Quito's international airport was conducted to determine the degree to which natural protected areas influenced tourists' travel plans and activities. After socio-demographic data were collected, visitors were asked how important protected areas were in their decision to visit the country, how many protected areas they visited, and what kinds of nature-oriented activities they engaged in during their trip.

WWF Airport Survey Results

Socio-demographic Information

Average age:	50.0 years, youngest 7, oldest 80 years old (N=63).
Average nights:	Average number of nights was 11.4; shortest stay was two nights, longest was 35 (N=77).
Family members:	Of the 79 tourists surveyed, 34 (43 percent) came with family members. Average was 2.4 total family members. The largest family was six people.
Expenditures:	Of the 79 tourists surveyed, 57 reported an average total expenditure of $3,131. The average daily expenditure was $304 (N=55). The highest was more than $9,999, and the cheapest vacation cost $250. Of the respondents to this question, 37 people reported an average expenditure of $1,072 for airfare.
Income:	The average family income was over U.S. $40,000.
Gender:	56 percent of respondents were men, 44 percent were women.
Nationality:	The nationality distribution of the survey respondents (N=79) was as follows: 62.0 percent North American, 22.8 percent European, 6.3 percent Colombian, 2.5 percent Honduran, 2.5 percent Jamaican, and 3.8 percent all other.

Protected Area and Nature-oriented Information

Parks and protected areas were the most important reason given by tourists for their visit to Ecuador:

Main reason	52%
Important, influenced decision	13%
Somewhat important	14%
Not important	17%
No response	4%

Few of the tourists to Ecuador had been there before- 84 percent were first-time visitors, while 16 percent were repeat tourists. The principal reasons that visitors came to Ecuador this trip were:

Natural history	76%
Sightseeing	49%
Cultural history	38%
Business	8%

Other reasons for travel, such as visiting friends and family and enjoying the sun/beaches/recreation, each got a 5 percent response. The high number of people who cite natural history as their principal reason for traveling to Ecuador reflects the dominance of travel to the Galapagos, and may reflect the way tours and activities there are "packaged."

The most common activities tourists enjoyed in Ecuador were nature-based, reflecting the importance of nature tourism to the country:

Birdwatching	65%
Wildlife observing	60%
Boat trips	48%
Botany	30%
Hiking/trekking	22%
Local cultures	22%
Jungle excursions	10%
Mountaineering	9%
Camping	3%
Hunting/fishing	1%

When asked to list what they liked most about their visit to Ecuador, 26 of 79 visitors surveyed highlighted the country's "islands." The "friendliness of the people" was listed in 18 surveys, and 17 visitors commented on Ecuador's "natural resources, features and beauty." Also mentioned by 14 visitors was the country's "wildlife." Of 79 visitors surveyed, no dislike was repeated by more than 6 visitors; these included: "pollution, noise and litter," "crime," and the "airport facilities and services."

B. Supply of Natural Protected Areas

Geographically, Ecuador is a small but highly biologically diverse country divided into four distinct zones: the Sierra Highlands, the Amazon Basin (or Oriente), the Pacific Coast Highlands, and the Galapagos Islands. Across these four regions is a wide variety of protected natural ecosystems.

Yasuní National Park

Yasuní National Park is located in the Napo Province in Northeastern Ecuador. It is Ecuador's largest protected area, 679,000 hectares, that remains in a mostly pristine state. Sizable populations of the endangered jaguar can still be found in the park. The greatest threat to this protected area is oil exploration.

Sangay National Park

Encompassing 370,000 hectares, Sangay National Park is located on the eastern slopes of the Eastern Andean Range and is one of the largest protected areas in Ecuador. Its unique geological and natural features make this park one of the most interesting for research. It also contains important archeological Inca ruins that enhance its cultural importance. Spontaneous colonization is a major threat to this area.

Cuyabeno Wildlife Reserve

This reserve is located in the Napo Province of the Northeastern Amazon and encompasses an area of 254,760 hectares. It contains a wealth of plant and animal species with great economic potential. With mostly lowland rain forests and numerous oxbow lakes, the reserve has great potential for nature tourism. Native groups in the area traditionally practice subsistence hunting. Threats to the reserve come from spontaneous colonization and oil exploration.

Machalilla National Park

Machalilla National Park spans an area of 40,259 hectares in Northwestern Ecuador in the province of Manabí. This park features the most important sample of Pacific dry forest remaining in Ecuador. The park is home to 119 species of birds, and it includes an important marine area with two main islands, La Plata and Salango. Machalilla also preserves part of Ecuador's cultural heritage in Agua Blanca, one of the major pre-Columbian archeological remains in coastal Ecuador. Among the

many threats to the park are unplanned human encroachment, fires
during the dry season, forest cutting for fuelwood and charcoal,
overgrazing by goats and cattle, and desertification.

Podocarpus National Park

Podocarpus National Park is found in the provinces of Loja
and Zamora-Chinchipe on the eastern slopes of the southern Andes,
and encompasses an area of 146,280 hectares. Podocarpus is named
after the only coniferous tree native to the Andes. While poorly
known, the park's wildlife includes the rare spectacled bear and
the elusive mountain tapir. High plant endemism makes this area
a very high conservation priority. Poaching and illegal forest
cutting threaten this park.

Cayambe-Coca Ecological Reserve

Situated on the eastern slopes of the Andes in northern
Ecuador, this ecological reserve covers 403,103 hectares. It
encompasses an incredible diversity of ecosystems, ranging from
the paramo highlands to lowland rain forest. With over 317
species of reptiles and amphibians, it is one of the most diverse
areas on earth. Although the area remains largely unexplored,
spontaneous colonization is a major threat.

Cotachachi-Cayapas Ecological Reserve

This reserve covers an area of 204,420 hectares on the
western slopes of the Andes in northern Ecuador. Because of its
isolation from the Amazon region, this is a biogeographically
unique area containing the Colombian-Pacific assemblage of plant
and animal species that characterize the western slopes of the
Andes. The reserve probably has very high levels of endemism.
Agroindustrial activities and human encroachment threaten this
ecological reserve.

The Ecuadorean Park Service and Fundación Natura are working
on a new national conservation strategy for protected areas.
This should guide new, innovative conservation and sustainable
development programs in Ecuadorean parks. Roughly one half of
Ecuador's protected areas have management plans, but official
funds are insufficient to implement them.

In terms of personnel, Galapagos has the highest number of
employees (65), followed by Sangay (23), Cayambe-Coca (17),
Cotopaxi (16), Machalilla (15), Cotocachi-Cayapas (14).

Tourist infrastructure varies among the park sites, as can be seen in the following table:

Table 3.

___

INFRASTRUCTURE WITHIN NATIONAL PARKS AND RESERVES
ECUADOR, 1987

	ACCESS ROADS	VISITOR CENTER	CABINS	NATURE TRAILS	CAMPING AREAS	PICNIC AREAS
El Boliche	X	X	-	X	-	X
Cajas	X	X	-	-	-	-
Cayambe-Coca	-	-	-	-	-	-
Churute	-	-	-	-	-	-
Cotacachi-Caya.	X	X	2	X	-	-
Cotopaxi	X	X	2	X	X	X
Cuyabeno	X*	-	1	X	-	-
Galapagos Isl.	X**	X	X	X	-	-
Machalilla	X	-	-	X	-	-
Pasochoa	X	X	-	X	-	X
Pichincha	X	-	-	X	-	-
Podocarpus	X	-	-	-	-	-
Pululahua	X	-	-	X	-	-
Sangay	X	-	-	X	X	-
Yasuní	X*	-	X	X	-	-

* River access (dugout canoe travel)
** Daily cruises and yacht cruises
Source: Wilson, 1987, p. 29

___

III. Impacts of Tourism to Protected Areas

A. Economic Activities Related to Nature Tourism

Few studies have been completed to calculate the economic impact of nature tourism. Economic activities can be evaluated, however, by looking at the nature tour industry as well as examining jobs directly and indirectly created at a few specific sites.

Ecuador has several travel agencies that offer nature tours. The largest of these, Metropolitan Touring, has been a catalyst in the nature tourism industry for promoting the Galapagos Islands since the early 1970s. They continue to offer tours to the Galapagos as well as other special interest tours. Among these tours are trips to the Amazon Basin area, birdwatching excursions, and Indian culture tours. All tours include top-notch naturalist guides and high-quality accommodations when possible.

Etnotur and Nuevo Mundo are travel agencies that promote Ecuador worldwide through their main international affiliations. Their itineraries of adventure and nature tourism include mountaineering, jungle excursions, and train travel to Pacific northwestern Ecuador. Etnotur also offer tours to the Galapagos and recently built a new hotel on San Cristobal, one of the islands. These agencies also use experienced guides who receive thorough training.

Hotel Crespo is a travel agency located in the colonial city of Cuenca, in the province of Canar, and is the only established agency in that region offering nature-oriented tourism. Crespo offers excursions to Cajas National Park; jungle tours to the province of Morona-Santiago, including river travel in dugout canoes and visits to the Shuar Indians; trips to Ingapirca; and mountain lodging and trekking at Albergue de Montana. The manager of the hotel generally accompanies the tours. He acquired his natural history information from visiting scientists and national park studies.

There are several nature-oriented establishments such as the Hotel Anaconda, a rustic jungle cabin-type hotel that offers excursions to the rain forest. The Flotel Francisco de Orellana, located on the Napo River in the Napo province, is a flat-bottomed floating hotel operated by Metropolitan Touring.

In terms of economic impact at each natural protected area, each area is distinct in the extent and kind of economic activity that tourism generates. Below are examples of economic activities at several of the protected areas.

Galapagos National Park

A great deal of economic activity is directly and indirectly related to tourism at the Galapagos. This activity can be seen on the international, national, and local levels. At the international level, not only is there extensive international air travel in and out of the Galapagos, but also, many of the tours are arranged by foreign travel agencies. Some of the guides are also from other countries.

At the national level, income is generated for the national park system through entrance fees to the Galapagos. Foreign tourists pay a much greater amount than nationals to visit the islands. This income goes to the national park service to be distributed among all Ecuadorean parks. Galapagos receives the biggest portion of this income, about 50 percent of the total fee income. Roughly 25 percent of the funds for Galapagos go to finance its tourism program, including operational costs for ticket sales, park guards, and three patrol boat operators.

As a result of nature tourism, the Gross National Product of the Galapagos Islands province is the highest in Ecuador. Income at the national level is also generated through the many Ecuadorean travel agencies that offer trips to the Galapagos. Many guides are also drawn from the mainland to work on the islands.

Local economic impacts of tourism include residents who work as guides or as crew on boats, or who own restaurants, snack bars, or souvenir shops. A few years ago, it was noted that, while fishing has traditionally been the main economic activity of the Galapagos, many former fishing boats have been remodeled into day-tour boats (Garces y Ortiz, 1984).

Cotopaxi National Park

The economic impact of Cotopaxi is minimal in both direct and indirect terms. The park's small entrance fee is inadequate for park maintenance. There is no economic activity within the park, and the nearest human settlements are at a distance of several kilometers along the main road. A few restaurants along this road and a couple of small food stands benefit to varying degrees from the tourism.

The restaurant closest to Cotopaxi is "Los Pinos," where tourists are the main customers and source of income. The owner believes that about 35 to 40 percent of the clientele who stop at his restaurant have visited the park. The Cienega Restaurant and Hotel also receives some business from tourists to the park. In fact, the owner has made arrangements with some of the tour operators who bring visitors to the volcano to stop at his establishment.

Cuyabeno Reserve

Cuyabeno is one of nine wildland areas designated for immediate attention by the Ecuadorean Department of National Parks (Estrategia Nacional de Conservacion, 1976). This Amazonian reserve covers an area of 254,760 hectares of humid tropical forest and swamp forest and harbors significant populations of manatees, freshwater dolphins, tapirs, caimans, giant armadillos, and several of the spotted cats and other species listed as rare or endangered. In addition, the reserve surrounds a legally recognized tribal reserve of several hundred Siona-Secoya Indians. A multitude of serious threats to the reserve, such as oil exploration, the advancing agricultural "front" made up of thousands of colonists, African oil palm plantations, and illegal hunting threaten the integrity of the unit.

Despite insufficient infrastructure, various tour companies are presently operating in the reserve, and Indians are becoming involved with the business. Nuevo Mundo conducts a five-day/four-night trip in which participants spend three nights on the Laguna Grande within the reserve and the fourth night in the Hotel Cofán in Lago Agrio. Etnotur operates a similar five-day/four-night tour as well as an eight-day tour that travels down the Río Aguarico and up the Río Cuyabeno, thus showing participants a great deal more of the Cuyabeno Reserve. For the shorter tours, Nuevo Mundo charges U.S. $450 per person, and the tourists sleep in tents. Etnotur charges U.S. $300 for the same tour, but the tourists must sleep in hammocks.

Two small houses and one larger house that have been built in the reserve are being used by the Universidad Católica as a research station. These houses are situated on a small parcel of land surrounded by ponds where the Siona Indians have traditionally hunted and fished.

The area near the Laguna Grande is considered one of the ideal locations within the reserve for expanding tourism infrastructure. Lodging for tourists is being constructed here by residents of the community of Siona de Puerto Bolívar. Two buildings will be constructed; the framework for one is already completed. Administrative headquarters will be located here as well as basic tourist services such as latrines, garbage disposals/incinerators, water wells, and reserve maps and signs. Guard posts will be established at six locations in the reserve to help maintain adequate control.

B. Positive and Negative Impacts of Nature Tourism

1. Conservation Activities and Environmental Education

Many protected areas provide important opportunities to expand environmental awareness among foreigners and nationals. An example is Pasochoa Protection Forest Reserve, operated by Fundacion Natura and located near Quito. The park's purpose is to strengthen environmental education and all visitors receive educational materials and guided services. Eighty percent of the visitors are nationals and 20 percent are foreigners. The majority of the visitors during the week are children, who often bring their parents back on the weekend (Yolanda Kakabadse, pers. comm.)

2. Negative Impacts

Litter, pollution and trail erosion seem to be the most frequently reported problems at most natural protected areas in Ecuador. Other problems, such as illegal hunting and fishing at Cotopaxi, are also reported.

On the Galapagos, although there are no comprehensive scientific studies have been conducted to date, specific environmental impacts from tourism have been noted by longtime residents as well as naturalist guides. It has been noted that the albatross at Punta Suarez, while formerly nesting right beside tourist paths, have lately been moving away from the paths. Sea lions on Isla Lobos seem to become increasingly nervous and aggressive towards tourists. Some "chase" after tourists who get too close taking pictures.

In addition, trail erosion has been reported on Bartolome, Caleta Tagus, Santa Fe, Plaza Sur, and Seymour Norte islands. Although forbidden, tourists often leave litter on the islands; this can be fatal to marine turtles, which have been reported to mistake plastic bags for jellyfish, one of their food sources, and to die when the bags block their digestive tracts. Black coral is also illegally collected and sold at local souvenir stores.

C. Sociocultural Considerations

Although sociocultural aspects are an important topic for tourism development and management, they were not a focal point of this study and were not thoroughly analyzed. However, a few sociocultural observations were made in the course of obtaining information on the economic and environmental impacts of tourism.

For example, in Ecuador, tourism and its promises for a higher standard of living have lured many mainland Ecuadoreans to the islands. This has created many problems. The population has been growing at an uncontrollably fast pace--about 12 percent annually. Local residents resent newcomers taking jobs on the islands. With this new influx as well as increased numbers of tourists, there are often shortages of basic foods at local shops. The influx of tourism money into the area has raised prices in the Galapagos, making it difficult for locals, especially those not involved in tourism.

IV. Obstacles and Opportunities for Growth

A. Obstacles for Growth

One constraint to the growth of nature tourism in Ecuador is a lack of infrastructure at some parks and reserves. Inadequate infrastructure is partly due to limited park budgets and partly due to the lack of publicity to draw other funding sources to these parks for infrastructure development. There is an overall lack in the promotion of most of the parks on mainland Ecuador. The Galapagos Islands receive a great deal of national and international attention, and many of Ecuador's other parks remain unknown.

B. Opportunities for Growth

Ecuador is already well known for the Galapagos, and tourism could be expanded to the mainland by links with Galapagos tourism. Tourism packages could be created that include a few days at the Galapagos and a few days at other Ecuadorean parks readily accessible from cities like Quito, Guayaquil, Riobamba, and Cuenca.

V. Cotopaxi National Park (Case Study #1)

A. General Description and Infrastructure

Cotopaxi National Park, created in 1975, is located in the Andes about 90 kilometers south of Quito. From Quito, the park is an easy one-hour drive on good roads. The park's main attraction is the Cotopaxi volcano (5,897 m), often described as one of the most beautiful volcanoes in the world. Apart from the volcano, the park's flora and fauna include excellent examples of paramo (tropical high-altitude tundra), the Andean condor, hawks, caracaras, Andean lapwings, and many others. Rabbits, deer, Andean foxes, and pumas are among the park's most common mammals.

The park has a visitor center that provides maps and information on the flora and fauna of the area. A basic natural history museum contains an exhibition of animals to be found in the park. Cotopaxi has basic cabins but no food or fuel supplies. Two A-frame cabins are available for park personnel, visiting researchers, and scientists. Cotopaxi National Park also includes nature trails and areas for camping and picnicking. As Table 3 indicates, the park has one of the most complete sets of infrastructure of the Ecuadorean park system; however, most of the infrastructure is basic.

B. Visitor Information to Date

Due to the park's close proximity to Quito and its easy accessibility, it is a well-liked weekend destination for many Quito families to have picnics and recreation. During the week, it is mostly visited by foreigners.

Peak season for national visitors is May through August, and for international visitors, January through April, with a smaller season in July and August.

According to the visitor register at Cotopaxi, (Table 4), visitation statistics show a decline in visitors over the past few years. Visitation has been declining by over 35 percent from 51,158 visitors in 1982 to 33,196 visitors in 1987. Data on the share of national versus international visitors are scarce, but the available figures show a moderate overall decrease for international visitors when comparing 1980 and 1987 figures. A considerable decrease in national visitors is therefore the main reason for declining numbers of visitors. While 39,504 Ecuadorean visitors came to see Cotopaxi National Park in 1980, the park attracted only 28,166 national visitors in 1987, or 32 percent less than in 1980.

Table 4.

COTOPAXI NATIONAL PARK
NATIONAL AND INTERNATIONAL VISITORS
1977 - 1987

YEAR	NATIONALS	%	INTERNATIONALS	%	TOTAL
1977	23,044	90.7	2,375	9.3	25,419
1978	25,345	87.7	3,574	12.4	28,919
1979	36,487	85.7	6,114	14.4	42,600
1980	39,504	88.4	5,208	11.6	44,712
1981	n.a.	n.a.	n.a.	n.a.	49,743
1982	n.a.	n.a.	n.a.	n.a.	51,158
1983	n.a.	n.a.	n.a.	n.a.	46,248
1984	n.a	n.a.	n.a.	n.a.	43,453
1985	n.a.	n.a.	n.a.	n.a.	47,279
1986	n.a.	n.a.	n.a.	n.a.	41,316
1987	28,166	84.8	5,030	15.2	33,196

Source: Visitor Registration, Cotopaxi National Park, 1988

C. Economic Impact

The economic impact of Cotopaxi is minimal in both direct and indirect terms. The park's small entrance fee is inadequate for park maintenance. There is no economic activity within the park, and the nearest human settlements are at a distance of several kilometers along the main road to the park. A few restaurants along this road and a couple of small food stands benefit to varying degrees from the tourism.

The restaurant closest to Cotopaxi is "Los Pinos," where tourists are a main income. The owner believes that about 35 to 40 percent of the clientele that stop at his restaurant have visited the park. The Cienega Restaurant and Hotel also receives some business from tourists to the park. In fact, the owner has made arrangements with several tour operators who bring visitors to the volcano to stop at his establishment.

D. Environmental Impact

As for negative environmental impacts of tourism, litter seems to be the main problem. Since the amount of litter, especially after weekends, consumes the park guards' time in cleanup, it detracts from their efforts being oriented to other

activities such as control of visitors or information. Some
drivers are reported to drive off of the park road, causing
damage to the park's flora. Illegal hunting and fishing are the
most difficult problems to control. These "unofficial" visitors
to the park cause more damage than anyone else. The park's
transportation and communication equipment is not sufficient to
gain control over this situation.

VI. Galapagos National Park (Case Study #2)

A. General Description and Infrastructure

Galapagos National Park, created in 1959, is the oldest and best protected park of the Ecuadorean park system. The park consists of 11 large islands and numerous tiny islands. The islands can be reached only by boat or airplane, and the majority of tourists arrive via air to the island of Baltra or to the island of San Cristóbal. From there they transfer to waiting cruise ships or buses and travel to the islands' capital, Puerto Ayora.

Airlines flying to the two airports are the military airline TAME (Baltra) that has daily flights with a passenger capacity of about 125 passengers, and the private airline SAN (San Cristobal). Baltra has a simple but well-constructed airport. Once arriving at Baltra, passengers take a bumpy three-hour bus ride to Puerto Ayora, the focal point for hotels and daily tours. The road to Puerto Ayora is often a difficult passage, dusty in the dry season and dangerous in the rainy season.

Several small hotels or pensions are found in Puerto Ayora and Puerto Baquerizo (San Cristobal Island). Most of them are geared towards national tourism. With the explosive increase of national visitors, small hotels and pensions have been burgeoning.

Table 5.

SUPPLY OF HOTEL ROOMS IN PUERTO AYORA PUERTO BAQUERIZO MORENO 1981 AND 1987

	CATEGORY	HOTELS		ROOMS	
		1981	1987	1981	1987
PUERTO AYORA	1	2	4	31	52
	2	4	7	92	99
	3	6	3	42	25
Subtotal		12	14	165	176
PUERTO	1	0	1	0	10
BAQUERIZO	2	2	7	2	59
	3	1	3	9	32
Subtotal		3	11	11	101
TOTAL		15	25	176	277

Source: Garcés y Ortiz, 1984; Moore, 1987.

96

Most tourists to the Galapagos, especially foreign tourists, do not stay in one of the local hotels but immediately transfer to a cruise ship after arriving in Baltra. These cruise ship tours last from three days to two weeks and generally visit between five and 11 islands.

Various small tour companies offer day tours to one or two islands on boats that accommodate up to 12 people. All these tours are accompanied by a local auxiliary guide. In total, 57 boats are operating in the Galapagos with a permit from the National Forestry Administration (DINA). There are three large cruise ships with capacities of 90 passengers; the remainder have capacity for two to 20 passengers. The three cruise ships actually monopolize over 50 percent of total annual passenger capacity (Moore, 1987). Total passenger capacity, based upon boat availability from January through June 1987, was given at 42,298 passengers; 39.3 percent of this capacity, or 16,603 passengers, actually used the boats.

In 1975, along with the park's management plan, an exemplary formal training system for tour guides was designed. The training is divided into two categories: naturalist guides and auxiliary guides. Naturalist guides need to have completed three years of university training or its equivalent in natural sciences, and be fluent in English. To obtain permission to work as a naturalist guide on the Galapagos Islands, guides have to participate in and pass an intensive one-month training course, held every year in September.

The course is organized by the park in cooperation with the Charles Darwin Research Station and contains over 30 lectures on the natural history of the islands, the theory behind national parks, and park organization and history. The course also includes group discussion and mandatory reading (Moore, 1981). Naturalist guides are permitted to lead groups of between 12 and 90 visitors. Auxiliary guides are permitted to lead groups up to 12 people.

The town has several basic restaurants and at least three grocery stores. Several souvenir shops sell post cards, tee-shirts, black coral, and other tourist items. A tourism information office is located in the center of town.

Set apart from the town is the Charles Darwin Research Center and the main building of the National Park Service. Within the Charles Darwin Research Center is a museum and a small zoo.

B. Visitor Information to Date

Traditionally, the Galapagos Islands have had more international than national visitors. As shown in Table 6, however, the share of national visitors has been gaining consistently over the past 20 years, with only one setback in 1985. Recently there has been a dramatic surge in national visitors; between 1985 and 1986, national arrivals almost doubled from 6,279 to 12,126. In contrast, international arrivals have been fairly stagnant since 1980. In 1987, for the first time, more national visitors were registered in the Galapagos National Park than international visitors.

Tourism influx to the Galapagos Islands has increased by over 335 percent from 7,500 visitors (1974) to 32,595 (1987). This increase has not been continuous, but rather has shown minor setbacks in 1976, 1979, 1981, and 1985. The considerable decrease experienced in 1976 might be related to the international economic crisis and a general lull in the international travel market. Tourism seems to have grown in leaps in 1978, 1980, and 1986, when figures jumped by about 50 percent in relation to the previous year. (Moore, 1987)

Many of these new arrivals, especially the nationals, can be attributed to the opening of a new airport on San Cristobal Island. Almost 6,000 additional visitors arrived at this airport in 1986 alone.

Table 6.

ANNUAL FLOW OF VISITORS
GALAPAGOS NATIONAL PARK
1974 - 1987

YEAR	NATIONAL	%	FOREIGN	%	TOTAL	% CHANGE
1974					7,500	
1975					7,000	- 6.7
1976	863	13.8	5,432	86.2	6,300	-10.0
1977	1,349	17.3	6,439	82.7	7,788	23.6
1978	1,606	13.1	10,693	86.9	12,299	57.9
1979	2,226	18.9	9,539	81.1	11,765	- 4.3
1980	3,980	22.8	13,465	77.2	17,445	48.3
1981	4,036	24.8	12,229	75.2	16,265	- 6.8
1982	6,067	35.4	11,056	64.6	17,123	5.3
1983	7,254	41.1	10,402	58.9	17,656	3.2
1984	7,627	40.4	11,231	59.6	18,858	6.8
1985	6,279	35.2	11,561	64.8	17,840	- 5.4
1986	12,126	46.6	13,897	53.4	26,023	45.9
1987	18,000	55.2	14,500	44.5	32,595	25.3

Source: Moore, 1987, p.10, Galapagos National Park Service.

It is necessary to note that the accuracy of official statistics has been questioned. Unofficial statistics indicate that in 1986, when the San Cristobal airport was opened, the islands were flooded by almost 50,000 visitors, far beyond the officially established carrying capacity limit of 25,000 visitors.

Table 7.

SALE OF NATIONAL PARK ENTRY TICKETS
SAN CRISTOBAL ISLAND
1986 - 1987

YEAR	NATIONALS	%	FOREIGNERS	%	TOTAL
1986*	4,162	71.5	1,655	28.5	5,817
1987**	5,139	68.4	2,369	31.6	7,508

---

* Not including January
** Only January-September
Source: Moore, 1987, p.14.

Seasonality patterns can be deducted from Table 8, with high season for national tourism in the months of April, May, August, and September. As for international visitors, they tend to concentrate January and August, and to a lesser extent in July and March. Absolute low season for international visitors is the month of September.

Table 8.

AVERAGE NUMBER OF NATIONAL, INTERNATIONAL, AND TOTAL MONTHLY
VISITORS TO GALAPAGOS NATIONAL PARK FROM 1979-1986

	AVG. NATIONAL	AVG. INTERNATIONAL	AVG. TOTAL
Jan	319.25	1424.38	871.81
Feb	394.63	952.00	673.31
Mar	476.75	1022.63	749.69
Apr	645.25	995.88	820.56
May	589.38	820.25	704.81
June	481.25	788.75	635.00
July	462.50	1098.88	778.19
Aug	761.63	1259.25	1010.44
Sept	778.38	630.00	704.19
Oct	525.13	854.13	689.63
Nov	387.13	972.75	679.94
Dec	378.13	858.63	618.38

Source: Moore, 1987

An analysis of total arrivals between July of 1986 and June
of 1987 reveals a dominance of U.S. visitors (28.7 percent) among
foreign visitors. Other significant groups include Germans (6.8
percent), Swiss (3.2 percent), Italians (3.1 percent), and
Canadians (2.7 percent). Surprisingly, visitors from other Latin
American countries total only 2.1 percent of arrivals (Tourism
Report II).

Most tourists to the Galapagos Islands, especially foreign
tourists, do not stay in one of the local hotels but immediately
transfer to a cruise ship after arriving at Baltra. These cruise
ship tours last from three days to two weeks and, depending on
itinerary, visit between five and 11 islands.

A study of visitor use by Moore (1987) comparing the
visitor use data of 1986-87 with 1979-80 visitor use information
came to the following interesting conclusions (see Table 9):

1. The increased use of Seymour Norte and Playa Las Bachas
(Baltra Island) as tour destinations can be deduced from the
increase in day tours and the increased use of Baltra Harbor to
meet and leave cruise ship tourists.

100

2.   There is a notable change in site visits to locations close
to Puerto Baquerizo Moreno on the island of San Cristobal.   In
1979-80, only 26 tourists visited Isla Lobos.   During 1986-87,
over 3,095 people or 2.2 percent of all visits were made to Isla
Lobos.   The reason for this was increased day tour tourism made
possible by the new San Cristobal airport.

3.   Frequent site visits are congruent with proximity to visitor
arrival points, especially those to Seymour Norte, Plaza Sur,
Bartolomé, Santa Fe, Rábida, Playa Las Bachas, and Isla Lobos.

Table 9.

VISITORS TO VARIOUS SITES: GALAPAGOS NATIONAL PARK
A COMPARISON

	TOTAL VISITORS 1979-80	% OF THE TOTAL SITES	TOTAL VISITORS 1986-87	% OF THE TOTAL SITES	% CHANGE
Pta. Suarez	9,399	7.7	9,576	6.7	1.9
Bahia Gardner	1,615	1.3	2,527	1.8	56.4
Isla Lobos	26	0.0	3,095	2.2	11,803.8
Pto. Grande	8	0.0	511	0.4	6,287.5
Sta. Fe	6,057	5.0	8,933	6.3	47.5
Plaza Sur	14,326	11.8	15,870	11.1	10.8
B. Conway	56	0.0	243	0.2	333.9
Playa Las Bachas	2,013	1.7	5,405	3.8	1,685.0
Caleta Tortuga	2,690	2.2	4,768	3.3	77.2
I. Mosquera	1,235	1.0	875	0.6	- 29.0
Daphne	1,043	0.8	1,090	0.8	4.5
Seymour Norte	11,851	9.8	15 966	11.2	34.8
B. Darwin	3,642	3.0	4,768	3.3	30.9
El Barranco	612	0.5	2,297	1.6	275.3
Bartolome	12,538	10.3	14,621	10.2	16.6
Bahia Sullivan	2,168	1.8	4,890	3.4	125.5
C. Bucanero	411	0.3	714	0.5	73.7
Playa Espumilla	7,085	5.8	1,784	1.2	- 74.8
Pto. Egas*	11,310	9.3	7,204	5.0	- 36.3
Sombrero Chino	2,541	2.1	3,626	2.5	42.7
Rabida	3,702	3.1	8,093	5.7	118.6
Pta. Espinosa*	6,752	5.6	5,441	3.8	- 19.4
Volcan Alcedo	314	0.3	593	0.4	88.8
Pta. Garcia	470	0.4	581	0.4	23.6
Pta. Albemarle	23	0.0	138	0.1	500.0
Pta. Tortuga	33	0.0	142	0.1	330.3
C. Tagus*	6,668	5.5	5,338	3.7	- 19.9
B. Urbina	69	0.1	409	0.3	492.8
B. Elizabeth	47	0.0	266	0.2	466.0
Pta. Moreno	56	0.1	232	0.2	314.3
Pta. Cormoran	8,522	7.0	7,028	4.9	- 17.5
B. Post Office	4,062	3.3	2,887	2.0	- 28.9
Corona del Diablo	....	...	2,613	1.8	....
Cerro Brujo	....	...	275	0.2	....

* For 1986-87, the number is low because of insufficient data
    Source: Moore, 1987

C. WWF Park Survey Results

Information on visitor profiles was obtained by WWF during two survey weeks,[1] when 64 international and 15 national[2] tourists were interviewed. Half of all visitors interviewed were North American, followed by Europeans (41 percent) and Australians (5 percent). A slight majority of visitors were male (55 percent); the mean age was 40 and the mean annual income close to U.S. $40,000. Visitors were generally accompanied by relatives (45 percent) or friends and colleagues (31 percent).

Main motivations for visiting the Galapagos Islands National Park were rare species (77 percent), its fauna (70 percent), its flora (42 percent), geology (42 percent), adventure (31 percent), and recreation (13 percent). Nature-related activities performed by tourists included hiking, wildlife observation, birdwatching, botany, and boat excursions.

Tourists used planes (83 percent), boats (63 percent) and buses (36 percent) to travel to and around the Galapagos Islands. Two-thirds of all visitors spent at least one night within the park, with the mean number of nights spent inside or near the park at eight. Over 83 percent of all surveyed used a boat or yacht as accommodation facility.

D. Economic Impact of Tourism to the Galapagos

A great deal of economic activity is directly and indirectly related to tourism at the Galapagos. At the international level, not only is there extensive international air travel in and out of the Galapagos, but also, many of the tours are arranged by foreign travel agencies.

At the national level, income is generated for the national park system through entrance fees to the Galapagos. Foreign tourists pay a much greater amount than nationals to visit the islands. This income goes to the National Park Service to be distributed among all Ecuadorean parks. The Galapagos Islands Park receives the biggest portion of this income, about 50 percent of total fee income. Roughly 25 percent of the funds collected for Galapagos go to finance its tourism program, including operational costs for ticket sales, park guards, and three patrol boat operators.

---

[1]One week in February (high season), and one week in July (low season).

[2]Due to the small group size for nationals, results from their surveys are disregarded in this section.

As a result of nature tourism, the GNP of the Galapagos Islands province is the highest in Ecuador. Income at the national level is also generated through the many Ecuadorean travel agencies that offer trips to the Galapagos. Many guides are also drawn from the mainland to work on the islands.

Local economic impacts of tourism include income to residents who work as guides, work as crew on boats, or own restaurants, snack bars, or souvenir shops. A few years ago, it was noted that while fishing has traditionally been the main economic activity of the Galapagos, many former fishing boats were being remodeled into day-tour boats (Garces y Ortiz, 1984).

E. Environmental Impact

A frequently mentioned change on the islands is the introduction of non-endemic species such as the goat and the rat. However, there is a dispute whether or not this is attributable to tourism or simply to human colonization of the islands. Tourism, according to some sources, is responsible for the introduction of the Norwegian rat and the red ant. Major efforts are being undertaken to rid the islands of these introduced species.

Scientific studies performed through the Charles Darwin Station have not shown noticeable impact on flora and fauna of the Galapagos Islands through current tourism. However, impacts have been noted by long-time residents as well as naturalist guides, and it can be deduced that they have occurred because of tourism. These include the following:

1. The albatross at Punta Suárez, while formerly nesting beside tourist paths, have been moving away from these routes.

2. Sea lions, both male and female, on Isla Lobos seem to have become increasingly nervous and aggressive towards tourists. Some "chase" after tourists who get too close when taking pictures.

3. Path erosion is becoming problematic on Bartolomé, Caleta Tagus, Santa Fé, Plaza Sur, and Seymour Norte.

4. Although it is strictly forbidden to leave trash on the islands or in the waters, such disposal still occurs. Some marine turtles have been reported to swallow plastic bags, mistaking them for jellyfish, and then die when the plastic blocks their digestive systems.

5. Some tourists seem unable to resist the urge to feed animals. For several years, this had a dramatic impact on some animals that got so used to being fed that, when the extra feeding was stopped, they were unable to locate their natural food sources. This situation has now been brought more or less under control.

6. Black coral is being sold in the souvenir shops in Puerto Ayora. Although most guides warn their groups that black coral should not be bought, it remains the island's prime local souvenir.

On the positive side, there is a great deal of environmental education on the Galapagos. The nationals are very proud of the islands, and many have learned about conservation through the islands.

CHAPTER 5

MEXICO

I. Status of Tourism Industry

A. History and Growth

Mexico is a country with a rich tourism tradition, enjoying a worldwide reputation as an international tourism mecca. The development of this industry in Mexico has shown an enormous, almost continuous growth from about 20,000 tourists in 1929 to more than 5,400,000 in 1987. As a result of this growth, tourism has been among the three leading sources of foreign exchange for the last 30 years.

Before the 1960s, most tourist activity focused on beach, "sun and fun" tourism in Acapulco and shopping tourism or border tourism in Tijuana. In the 1970s, spatial diffusion of tourism began, so that by the mid-1980s, Mexico's tourism industry was booming along the Pacific and Caribbean coasts and in Mexico City. The upward development of Mexican tourism in terms of number of visitors and foreign exchange generation has been interrupted only by the oil crisis and international recession of the mid-1970s and briefly by the earthquake of 1985.

This growth has been the consequence of an intensive national advertising effort by Mexican tourism agencies as well as the devaluation of the Mexican peso after 1976. The devaluation made traveling inexpensive for international visitors and also made traveling abroad expensive for nationals, thus turning their interest to local destinations. In the decade between 1976 and 1986, Mexican tourist arrivals increased by 48.9 percent from slightly over three million people to over four and a half million (1986) with an average annual rate increase of 4.4 percent.

Foreign exchange earnings for the same decade grew by over 114 percent from U.S. $835.6 million to U.S. $1,791.7 million (SECTUR,1987). A significant 82.6 percent, or U.S. $1,479.3 million, of the total corresponds to tourists arriving in Mexico by air. Average expenditures for these air tourists was U.S. $501, and for tourists entering by land, about U.S. $186. Therefore, mean expenditure was US $387 per foreign tourist in 1986. With an average length of stay of 9.9 days for the same year, the mean daily expenditures were U.S. $50.6 for air tourists and U.S. $18.8 for those arriving by land.

In 1986, tourism activity, including border transactions and international airfares, represented 17 percent of the current account revenues while expenditure in that sector contributed 9 percent. Tourism represented over 25 percent of non-petroleum exports. Tourism's contribution to the Gross Domestic Product (GDP) was estimated at 2.6 percent. (Tourism Report II)

Nearly 17,000 new direct and 42,000 new indirect jobs were created between 1983 and 1986 in the tourism sector. This increase brought the total working in the tourism sector in 1986 to over 1,800,000 (518,000 directly and 1,293,000 indirectly employed). Tourism-related employment in 1986 showed a 32 percent increase over the 1976 total employment figure of about 1,300,000. The 1986 total represented 7.3 percent of the economically active population (SECTUR).

In 1986, Mexico's international tourism was heavily dominated by its neighbor, the United States, with 84.2 percent of the total influx of tourists, followed by Canada (5.3 percent), Latin America (6.9 percent) and Europe (3.2 percent) (SECTUR). Air travel to Mexico showed a significant thrust in 1986 and increased almost 10 percent over the previous year.

Domestic tourism accounted for over 32 million travelers in 1986. These tourists stayed an average 1.9 days in hotels. Due to rising inflation and domestic travel costs, national tourists have had to modify their means of transportation, shifting predominantly to land transportation, which showed a 4 percent increase, while the number of Mexicans using domestic airlines decreased 11 percent (Tourism Report II).

B. Major Tourist Attractions

Mexico's tourist attractions are well known: a generally pleasant climate over most of its territory; beautiful beaches on both coasts with an adequate hotel infrastructure; colorful villages and towns; an outstanding archeological heritage, and a lesser known attraction--spectacular natural resources.

Geographically, Mexico's tourist attractions can be seen in five regions: the northwest, northeast, west-central, central, and southeast. Northwest Mexico comprises primarily Baja California, Sonora, and Chihuahua. The Copper Canyon in Chihuahua is a popular tourist attraction primarily because of the Taramara Indians. The long, jagged peninsula of Baja California is one of Mexico's most sparsely settled regions. For many years, it has attracted independent travelers who want a remote vacation. However, with the completion of the Trans-Peninsular Highway in 1973, tourism there is expanding. In addition to the fishing attraction, many tourists come to watch the grey whales. Tourism is rapidly becoming Baja California's largest industry.

Coahuila, Nuevo Leon, and Tamaulipas are the three border states that make up the northeast region. In this region, the greatest tourist attraction is Monterrey, the capital of Nuevo Leon. Monterrey is the third largest city in Mexico and is the nation's most important industrial center. Many U.S. citizens are attracted to this region to hunt doves.

In west-central Mexico is Mazatlan, an old port city that is becoming increasingly popular with both national and international tourists. The city is located on a rugged peninsula facing the Pacific and offers several good beaches, surfing, and excellent fishing facilities.

Also in this region, the state of Jalisco is becoming one of the country's busiest tourist centers. Guadalajara, its capital, is the second largest city in Mexico and has a colonial atmosphere and an excellent climate. Also in Jalisco is Lake Chapala, Mexico's largest lake and a retirement area for people worldwide.

The central region of Mexico is not only the most important area, economically and politically, but also the most important area traditionally for tourists. Among the attractions are the colonial city of Guanajuato; San Miguel de Allende, the artists' mecca; the silver capital of Mexico, Taxco; and the well-known port and resort area of Acapulco. However, the most significant tourist center in this region is Mexico City, the capital of the country. Mexico City has many famous museums, commercial zones, cathedrals, and parks that draw thousands of visitors each year.

In the southeast region is the state of Oaxaca, with its many important coastal resort areas, including Puerto Escondido, Puerto Angel, and the most recent development, Huatulco. At the southernmost end of the country is the state of Chiapas. Chiapas contains the Lacandon jungle, the largest rain forest remaining in North America. In addition to lush jungles and rugged mountain ranges, the state also has many Mayan ruins. The Yucatan Peninsula is also in this region. The Yucatan's primary attractions are its archeological sites, the flamingo colonies of Rio Celestun and Rio Lagartos, the Sian Ka'an Biosphere Reserve, and the resort area of Cancun.

Given this wide range of natural and cultural resources, Mexico is still best known to tourists as a sun and beach destination. Most natural protected areas in Mexico have yet to gain much national and international recognition as tourist attractions. Yet the country encompasses a wealth of natural features--varied landscapes, vegetation, and wildlife--that have enormous tourism potential.

Mexico has many unique natural resources. Its geographical location (it is the only nation in the world where the two great biogeographic regions, the Nearctic and the Neotropical, merge) and its complex physiography (the product of a dynamic geological history) give the country a dramatic biotic diversity.

Mexico has a richness and variety of plant and animal species that rivals anything found in the rest of North America, despite Mexico's territorial extensiond being one tenth the size of the remainder of the continent. In a recent study on biological diversity, Russell Mittermeier (1986) identified countries across the world that contain the highest diversity of plants and animals. Mexico is included in the six "mega-diversity" countries. The country has, for example, about 30,000 species of flowering plants, the highest number of mammals in all neotropical countries (439 species), more than 1,000 bird species, and the world's richest herpetofauna (957 species).

C. Tourism Policies, Promotion, and Management

The government of Mexico uses two principal bodies to regulate and promote tourism development. They are Fondo Nacional de Fomento al Turismo (FONATUR), or the National Trust Fund for Tourism Development, and the Sectretaria de Turismo (SECTUR), which is the Ministry of Tourism.

FONATUR was established in 1974 to supply financial support, at preferential interest rates, for the construction of hotels, tourist condominiums, restaurants, and other tourism facilities. FONATUR has played a significant role in the development of some major tourist centers in Mexico, including Cancun, Ixtapa, Los Cabos, Loreto, and most recently, Huatulco.

In addition to creating new tourist centers, FONATUR has a program that grants credit to expand, remodel, or build hotels and other tourist facilities. Since 1974, this program has financed more than 128,000 new rooms, which is 85 percent of the hotel rooms built in the country since that time. The trust fund authorized 172 credit operations in 1986. Through this financial support, the construction of more than 5,000 new rooms and the remodelling of an additional 4,000 rooms was undertaken. It is estimated that the construction of the new rooms directly or indirectly created over 13,000 jobs (Tourism Report II).

This increase in hotel capacity is significant to the tourism industry. In 1986, Mexico had more than 275,000 rooms in almost 7,000 establishments. In addition to these conventional hotels, there are another 30,000 unconventional rooms in places such as pensions, boarding houses, and villas. (Tourism Report II).

In addition to supplying funds for accommodation projects, FONATUR is also responsible for the majority of tourism's promotion in Mexico. This agency takes the lead in publicity and advertising for the tourism industry.

The other federal agency that plays a significant role in the tourism industry is SECTUR. In February, 1984, the Federal Law of Tourism established SECTUR as the federal agency in charge of regulating tourism activity in the country and coordinating the plans of the tourism offices of the different state governments. SECTUR carries out this mandate through a variety of different mechanisms. SECTUR's National Register of Tourism is a clearinghouse of available tourism services nationwide. The Center of Higher Studies in Tourism is a branch of SECTUR that deals with research and training programs for people in the tourism industry. Also, SECTUR handles international cooperation agreements to exchange information about tourist activities.

There are indications that the government will begin to more actively promote tourism to protected natural areas. One indication is seen in the government's 1988 publication called "The General Law for Ecological Balance and Environmental Protection," which frequently mentions the advantages of tourism to the national parks and the need to develop nature tourism.

II. Status of Tourism to Protected Areas

A. Demand for Tourism to Protected Areas

Although tourism in general has been a major industry in Mexico for many years, the segment of tourism to protected areas is just beginning to expand. In the last few years, increasing numbers of foreigners and nationals are discovering the extraordinary natural resources of Mexico.

One objective of the present study was to gather information on the increasing demand for nature tourism in Mexico. This was achieved primarily by gathering existing data about numbers of tourists to protected areas from tour operators and from recorded park statistics. Secondarily, surveys of general tourists were conducted at an international airport to determine what proportion of the tourists cite natural history as an important factor in their decision to come to Mexico and what proportion cite protected areas as their main reason to come to Mexico.

Very little has been written about the nature tourism trend in Mexico. In 1985, a review of several popular nature magazines identified 36 travel agencies specializing in ecological tourism (frequently combined with cultural tourism) that advertised their nature tours. Of these 36 agencies only 12 (nine from the U.S., two from Canada, and one from within Mexico) offered ecological excursions, predominantly ornithological, in Mexico. The agencies combined offered a total of 56 nature tours to Mexico in 1985. (Olmsted, 1985).

Visitor statistics vary greatly at protected sites in Mexico and in many cases, it is difficult to document the trends of nature tourists. However, there are a few examples to demonstrate the increasing numbers at parks and reserves.

The Monarch Butterfly Reserve, dedicated to protect the overwintering sites of the monarch butterfly, has seen an enormous explosion in number of visitors. Located outside Mexico City in the mountains that border the states of Mexico and Michoacan, visitation to the reserve increased from 9,000 visitors in 1984-85 to 70,000 visitors in 1987-88. (SEDUE, 1988).

Although there are no official records for the total number of tourists that visit Izta-Popo National Park, the number of tourists that stay overnight has been recorded, and there has been a gradual, upward trend.

Table 1.

OVERNIGHT GUESTS AT VICENTE GUERRERO MOUNTAIN LODGE
IZTA-POPO NATIONAL PARK
1984-1987

YEAR	TOTAL	NATIONALS	in %	FOREIGNERS	in %
1984	10,993	7,717	70.2	3,276	29.8
1985	10,998	7,471	67.9	3,527	32.1
1986	13,097	9,740	74.4	3,357	25.6
1987	14,538	10,796	74.3	3,742	25.7
Total	49,626	35,724	72.0	13,902	28.0

Source: Vicente Guerrero Mountain Lodge visitor registration

The increase in tourism to protected areas can also be seen
in the visitation statistics at Sumidero National Park, one of
the few parks where consistent statistics have been recorded.

Table 2.

SUMIDERO NATIONAL PARK VISITATION STATISTICS 1983-1987

YEAR	TOTAL VISITORS	NATIONALS (%)		FOREIGN (%)		TOTAL INCREASE	(%)
1983	72,384	67,548	(93.3)	4,836	(6.7)	- - -	- - -
1984	83,317	76,096	(91.3)	7,221	(8.7)	10,933	(15.1)
1985	85,005	77,292	(90.9)	7,713	(9.1)	1,688	(2.0)
1986	105,660	94.843	(89.8)	10,817	(10.2)	20,655	(24.3)
1987	129,318	110,196	(85.2)	19,122	(14.8)	23,658	(22.4)
Total	475,684	425,975	(89.5)	49,709	(10.5)	56,934	(78.7)

Source: SEDUE, Chiapas

Surveys of tourists were conducted at the airport in Mexico City to determine the degree to which natural protected areas influenced tourists' travels plans and activities. After socio-demographic information was established, visitors were asked how important protected areas were in their decision to visit the country, how many protected areas they visited, and what kinds of nature-oriented activities they participated in during their t ip.

WWF Airport Survey Results

Socio-demographic Information

Average age:	42.3 years, youngest 16, oldest 74 years old (N=69).
Average nights:	Average number of nights was 15.7; shortest stay was two nights, longest was 99+ (N=67).
Family members:	Of the 71 tourists surveyed, 26 (37 percent) came with family members. Average was 2.7 people, or closer to three family members. The largest family group was six people.
Expenditures:	The average total expenditure per trip to Mexico was $1,919 (N=65), while the average daily expenditure was $237. The highest total vacation cost was $8,800, and the cheapest vacation cost $500. Of the respondents, 53 people reported an average expenditure of $543 for airfare.
Income:	The average family income range was between U.S. $30,000 and $40,000.
Gender:	49 percent were men, 51 percent were women.
Nationality:	The nationality distribution of the survey respondents (N=71) was as follows: 49.3 percent North American, 21.1 percent European, 5.6 percent Mexican, 4.2 percent French, 2.8 percent Colombian, 2.8 percent Venezuelan, 2.8 percent Argentine, and 11.4 percent all other.

Protected Areas and Nature-oriented Tourism

Parks and protected areas were cited as important in influencing tourist decisions to visit Mexico in the following proportions:

Main reason	24%
Important, influenced decision	18%
Somewhat important	18%
Not important	38%
No response	2%

The majority of visitors, 62 percent, had previously visited Mexico. The top five reasons for the present trip were:

Sightseeing	38%
Sun/beaches/recreation	37%
Visit friends or family	35%
Cultural history	23%
Archeology	18%

Relatively few tourists in Mexico participated in activities that reflect an orientation to wildlands, jungles, or natural history. The importance of beaches and sightseeing in the decision to visit Mexico, as well as its rich cultural activities are what most tourists enjoy:

Local cultures	37%
Boat trips	17%
Hiking/trekking	11%
Hunting/fishing	10%
Mountaineering	10%
Wildlife observing	9%
Jungle excursions	7%
Camping	4%
Birdwatching	1%
Botany	1%

Visitors were asked to list what they liked and disliked most about their visit to Mexico. The "friendliness of the people" was mentioned as most liked by 45 of the 71 visitors surveyed. Twenty-three visitors listed "food and restaurants," and 11 highlighted the "climate." Among the most frequently listed dislikes were Mexico's "pollution, noise and litter," recorded in 36 of 71 surveys, and its "road system and lack of road signs," recorded by 10 visitors.

B. Supply of Protected Areas

1. Development and Management of Park System

Mexico has a great variety of categories for protected natural areas. The variation in name, objectives, and management is confusing and difficult to distinguish. In the 96 protected areas that have been declared to date, there are 26 distinct denominations. Among these denominations are:

"Parks"
-national park
-natural park
-recreation and cultural park
-marine park

"Reserves"
-reserve
-natural reserve
-hunting and fishing reserve
-biosphere reserve

"Protected Zones"
-protected forest zone

"Refuges"
-national wildlife refuge
-marine refuge
-migratory bird refuge

"Natural Protected Area"
-natural protected area

(Source: Fauna Silvestre y Areas Naturales Protegidas, 1988)

Although the government has reported to have protected nearly 2.5 percent of the territory in these areas, only 0.8 percent of the country is actually protected.

The Mexican government recently passed the "General Law of Ecological Balance and Environmental Protection" (1988) to state the importance of the protected areas that together make up the National System of Protected Areas (Sistema Nacional de Areas Naturales Protegidas or SINAP). The main functions of the protected areas system, administered by the Ministry of Urban Development and Ecology (SEDUE), is to "promote and conserve the natural richness of the country, introducing visitors to the knowledge of the vital values found in nature and the need for its protection to benefit present and future generations." (Ley

General del Equilibrio Ecologico y la Proteccion al Ambiente, 1988).

Although the new law outlines yet another set of categories for protected areas, there is consensus among all statistics that the total number of national parks in Mexico is 44. Many of these parks are located near large cities and receive many visitors, although no firm statistics are kept. The majority of visitors to these parks, however, are not "hard-core" nature tourists, but rather go to the parks on day excursions for recreation.

2. Examples of Protected Natural Areas

Constitucion de 1857 National Park

Located in the Sierra de Juarez, Constitucion de 1857 is just over 5,000 hectares and is primarily pine-oak forest. Established in 1962, it has several lakes, the largest one being Juarez Lake. The park hosts many endangered species, including the mule deer, bighorn sheep, bald eagle, coyotes, osprey, and pinyon jays. Facilities at the park include an office, a visitor center, a lodge with 13 rooms, camping sites, guard's cabin, picnic facilities, and a parking area.

Lagunas de Montebello National Park

In the state of Chiapas, Lagunas de Montebello has 52 lakes and covers over 6,000 hectares. Established in 1959, the park has pine-oak and cloud forest, with an abundance of ferns and orchids. Wildlife includes: brocket deer, tayra, ocelot, quetzal, black chachalaca, azure-naped jay, barred parakeet, and the blue-crowned chlorophonia. In addition to the natural resources, there are also some archeological sites.

The park has picnic facilities, overlooks, trails, a basic tourist lodge, and a camping area. Sightseeing boats can be leased to tourists. Swimming and snorkeling are allowed in some lakes.

Palenque National Park

Declared a national park in 1981, Palenque is only 1,772 hectares in the state of Chiapas. Despite its small size, the park contains many extraordinary cultural and natural resources. The world-famous site of Palenque from the classic Maya period is in the park. The park also has spectacular rain forest with a great diversity of wildlife. Fauna includes: toucans, woodpeckers, motmots, antbirds, parrots, crested currassow, howler monkey, ocelot, and anteaters. Palenque is considered by many to be the best spot in Mexico for birdwatching.

Tourist facilities at Palenque are a parking lot, park headquarters, restrooms, trails, and a small archeological museum. There are several hotels near the park.

Cascada de Basaseachic National Park

Located in Chihuahua, Cascada de Basaseachic was established in 1981. This 5,802-hectare park protects the highest waterfall in Mexico (310 m) as well as an ecosystem representative of the northern Sierras. It has canyons, mountain streams, and pine-oak forest. Fauna includes: white-tailed deer, coyote, mountain lion, golden eagle, peregrine falcon, woodpeckers, and ocellated quail. The physical infrastructure at the park is minimal, with only a picnic area and primitive camping facilities.

Lagunas de Zempoala National Park

In Morelos, the state of Mexico, is the Lagunas de Zempoala National Park. Covering 4,669 hectares, it dates to 1936. The park contains volcanic terrain, with pine, oak, and fir forests as well as six mountain lakes. Flora includes: alders, willows, heaths, and other wild flowers. Fauna includes: white-tailed deer, bobcats, skunks, rabbits, hawks, woodpeckers, juncos, hummingbirds, and swallows as well as several species of reptiles and amphibians.

Permits can be obtained from SEDUE to fish or camp in the park. There are also picnic facilities, restrooms, eateries, and an amusement area for children.

Cumbres de Monterrey National Park

Located in the state of Nuevo Leon, Cumbres de Monterrey is the largest national park in Mexico. Also one of the oldest, the park was created in 1939 and measures 246,500 hectares. The park contains barrancas, canyons, scenic ridges, geological formations, arroyos, caves, and waterfalls. Vegetation is composed of pine-oak forest, submontane scrub, tropical deciduous vegetation, and desert chaparral. Wildlife includes: opossums, jackrabbits, peccaries, raccoons, coati, skunks, mountain lions, hawks, crimson-collared grosbeak, and many species of reptiles and amphibians.

The park functions as an important hydrographic basin, supplying Monterrey with its water. There are many tourist facilities at Cumbres de Monterrey throughout the park. Visitors come for a variety of activities including mountain climbing, horse-back riding, camping, and speleology.

Sian Ka'an Biosphere Reserve

The Sian Ka'an Biosphere Reserve is on the Caribbean Coast of the state of Quintana Roo. It covers 528,174 hectares of tropical evergreen forest, marshes, mangroves, extensive sea grass beds, freshwater lagoons, and marine and reef environments. The Sian Ka'an Biosphere Reserve is often cited as one of the best Latin American examples of the new approach to natural area protection that seeks to integrate conservation with the development needs of surrounding rural populations.

Activities on the reserve include El Ramonal Agricultural Plot which is designed to experiment with and demonstrate ecologically appropriate farming methods on the poor soils of the Yucatan, the spiney lobster postlarval recruitment study, a palm ecology and management project and extension work by an environmental educator with communities surrounding the reserve. An ecotourism project is just beginning to promote and manage tourism to the reserve.

III. Impacts of Tourism to Protected Areas

A. Economic Activities Related to Nature Tourism

To date, there are no national statistics on employment related directly and indirectly to nature tourism. However, there are many parks and reserves that offer significant employment opportunities in tourism to both the local population and to outside tour groups using the natural area. A few examples of the level and kinds of employment generated in parks and reserves follows.

Monarch Butterfly Ecological Reserve

With the recent establishment of the Monarch Butterfly Reserve in 1986, and the great increase in tourists to the reserve, many residents of the local community have begun working in the tourist business. With the help of Monarca, a Mexican non-governmental organization, a visitors center, a snack bar, and a gift shop have been built. Trails with interpretive signs have also been developed. Trail guides have been trained. The local residents, who had previously logged the area and threatened the monarch habitat, are now profiting from the tourists and maintaining the natural resources of the area. They have made a transition in their livelihood from a resource-destructive activity to a resource-sustaining activity.

The economic impact of tourism to the reserve can also be seen in the town closest to it. There are no overnight facilities at the reserve, but many tourists stay in nearby Angangueo, an old silver-mining town. In addition to the increased demand for accommodations, residents of the town also often supply transportation to the reserve. The reserve is located in the mountains about an hour's drive from Angangueo. Therefore, many people in the town are gaining income from driving visitors to the reserve.

Izta-Popo National Park

Situated 80 kilometers outside Mexico City, Izta-Popo Park centers around the imposing, perpetually snow-clad volcanic peaks of Iztaccihuatl (5,386 m) and Popocatepetl (5,542 m), the second and third highest mountains in Mexico.

There is no entrance fee to the park, but there is a minimal entrance fee (under U.S. $1) at the lodge for overnight visitors. The main economic activity is the park is the restaurant inside the lodge, which has a seating capacity of 150. It operates with nine employees during the week and 15 on the weekends. On the

weekends, the restaurant easily serves 1,000 meals. The
restaurant space is concessioned from the park and, therefore,
the owner pays rent to the park.

Also in the lodge, there is a small area where post cards,
pins, and posters are sold. Mountain climbing gear can also be
rented for a minimal price.

SEDUE employs about 35 people to maintain the park. This
includes a park manager, technical advisor, park guards, and
people working at the lodge and in the laundry.

Other economic activities related to the tourism at Izta-
Popo can be seen outside the park. Just before the park
entrance, there are several stands where foods and beverages are
sold. There is also some economic impact to the closest town to
the park. The town of Amecameca is 22 kilometers from Izta-Popo,
and some park visitors spend the night there. A more significant
impact is the number of local taxis that are hired at the bus
terminal in Amecameca to take visitors up to the mountains.

Sumidero Canyon National Park

As in other national parks, no entrance fee is charged to
visitors. Fourteen park guards and a park manager are employed
by SEDUE to maintain the area. There are no economic activities
on the park grounds that contribute to the park budget.

Three tourist services operate inside the park, although
none of them is concessioned to the park. Income is gained
through a restaurant at the Los Chiapa Lookout, which is
concessioned to the state government; a newer restaurant on the
riverside, owned and operated by workers of the Comision Federal
de Electricidad; and a tourist boat service.

The nearby city of Tuxtla Gutierrez receives some economic
impact, although this is difficult to quantify. Tuxtla Gutierrez
receives a great number of visitors, but how many of them have
been to Sumidero has not been calculated. There are many travel
and tour agencies in Tuxtla; some of them offer trips to
Sumidero.

B. Environmental Impacts

1. Conservation Activities and Environmental Education

There have been many positive environmental impacts from
tourism to protected areas. Protected areas provide the
opportunity for environmental education to increase the awareness

among national and international visitors of the value of natural resources. Nature tourism has also increased the activities of some conservation organizations. Nature tourism has become a tool for many of these organizations to achieve their objectives.

Nature tourism is having an increasing influence on the conservation movement in Mexico. While conservationists have traditionally tried to minimize tourism to protected areas, they are becoming more aware of the conservation value of nature tourism.

Amigos de Sian Ka'an, A.C. is promoting the establishment of ecotourism circuits in the biosphere reserve and is investigating the creation of an ecological tourism center there.

Monarca, A.C., a non-governmental conservation organization created solely to protect the overwintering sites of the monarch butterfly, immediately recognized the need to integrate the local population into this goal. From the start, nature tourism became the new source of income for the surrounding rural population who had previously logged the area. Monarca, A.C. has also created an environmental education packet for children. This material has been distributed to many schools to inform them about the reserve and its conservation work.

INAINE (Instituto Autonomo de Investigaciones Ecologicas) has recently proposed the creation of a research station and Ecocultural Tourism Center in Palenque National Park in conjunction with the Laboratory of Ecology of the National Autonomous University of Mexico and Turismo Ecologico Mexicano.

CIPAMEX (the Mexican section of the International Council for Bird Preservation) has shown interest in the possibility of promoting bird tourism in the Chimalapas Reserve in the state of Oaxaca.

PRONATURA A.C. was created in 1981 to promote sound conservation of natural resources through educational activities, establishment of protected areas, and encouraging better laws for wildlife protection. In 1988 a Yucatan chapter was formally created. PRONATURA - Yucatan has been actively involved with nature tourism issues on the Yucatan Peninsula. They are hosting a meeting in April, 1989 to discuss tourism promotion and management with many national and international people from the tourism industry and conservation community.

2. Negative Impacts

In the majority of parks and reserves, few very serious environmental impacts have been observed to date, yet some minor problems could become major if not corrected. Also, in most cases, thorough studies on tourism's long-term impacts on plants and animals have not been conducted. Environmental carrying capacity figures have not yet been established, which makes it difficult to calculate the extent of these negative impacts. A sampling of some of the most serious and common problems encountered follows.

a. At Cascada de Agua Azul in Chiapas, much of the waste from tourist facilities is thrown directly into the river, affecting the water's natural blue color.

b. In Izta-Popo National Park, there is a variety of environmental problems. Garbage is often thrown along trails and alpine refuges, up to the summit of the volcanoes. Tourists also cause fires in the park. Another problem is the degradation of the water quality of the spring just below the lodge as a result of lack of refuse treatment at the lodge.

c. In the Piedras Encimadas de Zacatlan in Puebla and Basaseachic Falls in Chihuahua, a profusion of graffiti covers the boulders, cliffs, and other geological features that are among the main tourist attractions in these two areas.

d. In Lagunas de Montebello in Chiapas, orchids are reportedly picked in great numbers by tourists.

e. Disturbances of wildlife have been reported in some areas. Reports include: disturbance of grey whales by tour boats in the sanctuaries of Baja California, disturbance of flamingos in the reserve in Celestun, Yucatan, also from tour boats, and disruption of birds and howler monkeys by tour buses in Palenque National Park.

C. Sociocultural Considerations

Sociocultural impacts of tourism to protected areas are important to consider in making planning decisions about tourism's growth. This issue was not a focal point of the present study, however, and a complete analysis of sociocultural impacts is not presented. However, during the course of this study many sociocultural observations were noted. Some significant sociocultural issues are emerging as local populations are integrated into the tourism industry and provided with an alternative source of income or are displaced as a result of tourism development.

In the case of Sumidero Park, land tenure has been a severe problem for the park. When the park was decreed in 1980, twelve "ejidos" and some 300 private lots were left within the expropriated zone. Most of the private landowners, who apparently did not live off the land, were willing to accept indemnity and move out. But so far, no money has been available

to pay them. In the case of the "ejidatarios," who do live off
the land, very few have been compensated. This situation has
been a constant source of conflict, both social and economic,
reaching political significance.

Because of this unresolved land tenure problem, more and
more land inside the national park is being cleared for
agriculture and grazing. SEDUE technicians are now suggesting a
redefinition of park boundaries, reducing them so as to allow
more effective vigilance and to exclude areas that are
irreversibly damaged. At Sumidero Park, the park itself is being
threatened because of a lack of employment opportunities for the
surrounding communities which depend on the land.

IV. Obstacles and Opportunities in Nature Tourism's Development

A. Obstacles to Growth

There are several constraints to the growth of protected area tourism in Mexico. One problem is that most parks are not sufficiently funded, resulting in shortfalls in park maintenance and a lack of tourist services. Since parks do not generate income from entrance fees and most earn very little from the existing tourist facilities, parks are dependent on the government for funds. Since this funding is usually insufficient, parks lack adequate guards as well as facilities to attract tourists. The legal, managerial, and fiscal mechanisms are not yet in place to allow parks to operate effectively and to sustain a tourism industry.

Part of this financial problem can be explained by the budgeting system currently in place for the national parks. Income that parks generate from concessions, parking fees, or lodge fees is sent to the Ministry of Finance as internal revenue. Each year, the Ministry of Programming and Budget allots a budget to SEDUE to operate the national park system. Money programmed for each park is not based on the revenue that each brings in—in other words, the number of tourists who visit each park. A self-financing budgetary mechanism would be more helpful in redirecting funds to parks that need them.

Another factor that contributes to this overall lack of funds for parks is the limited sources of revenues for parks. Most parks do not charge entrance fees. Although not necessary at all parks, entrance fees could be an important source of income for the park system. A system of differential fees could be set up for nationals and foreigners.

Another legal issue that affects the parks' viability and ability to sustain tourism is inadequate demarcation of park boundaries. The status of some protected areas is very indefinite with respect to park limits, land tenure and land use rights, and management regulations; many parks are under severe pressures from local poor rural populations.

Further constraints to the ecotourism industry include: the current lack of infrastructure facilities for tourists; information available about tourists sites, including brochures and guide books; a lack of trained guides; and a lack of sufficient advertising or promotion of the ecotourism industry.

B. Opportunities for Growth

Given its enormous diversity and richness of natural attractions, Mexico has an outstanding nature tourism product. This is a key component in the success of tourism's growth.

Mexico also has the advantage of two important tourism markets close to its borders, the United States and Canada. Both countries already represent a significant portion of Mexico's general tourism, and both also have many nature enthusiasts in their citizenry pointing to the likelihood that demand could be increased for tourism to protected areas.

Thirdly, Mexico now has a worldwide reputation as a travel destination and a high level of general tourism. Efforts by states like Chiapas, Oaxaca, and the Yucatan Peninsula are being made to attract nature tourists. For these tourists, substantial infrastructure is already in place. Airports, communication services, and tourist facilities in the major cities can be used for a portion of nature tourists' trips, and new infrastructure development need take place only at the nature sites. In addition, the large numbers of tourists to Mexico provides a group of potential nature tourists that could "add-on" a nature trip to other travel plans. Therefore, nature tourism could constitute an additional tourist asset to the country. Nature tourism could serve to diversify Mexico's well-known cultural-historic-beach attractions.

V. Izta-Popo National Park (Case Study #1)

A. General Description and Infrastructure

Located 80 kilometers east of Mexico City, Izta-Popo National Park centers around the imposing, perpetually snow-clad volcanic peaks of Popocatépetl (5,542 m) and Iztaccíhuatl (5,386 m), the second and third highest mountains in Mexico.

To reach the park, travelers pass through fir forests from about 2,700 m to 3,300 m altitude. From there on, pine trees dominate the forests to an altitude of about 4,000 meters (the highest altitude where pine is found in the world). The park's entrance is marked by a building, but has no guard; consequently there is no record of visitors entering and leaving the park.

There is another gate about one kilometer beyond the entrance where there is a natural spring that supplies water for the park facilities. Shortly after this gate is the historical Paso de Cortes that marks the place where Cortez passed between the two mountains enroute to Tenochtitlan.

The paved entrance road leads to several parking areas, and then to the Vicente Guerrero Mountain Lodge (altitude 3,900 m). The mountain lodge is a well-designed building with a sloping red roof, owned and operated by SEDUE. The main lodge has four large bunk rooms with 98 beds, some meeting areas, living quarters for park personnel, and a restaurant that seats 150. There is also an older section of the lodge that has an additional 76 beds.

Other infrastructure includes a cabin with first-aid equipment, picnic grounds, and several mountain trails leading to the summits of the mountains.

B. Visitor Information to Date

High season at Izta-Popo is between October and March. Low season is from April through September, which coincides with the rainy season as well as with a lower level of tourism in Mexico in general. The park is heavily visited on weekends, with an estimated average of 500 cars; only a few tourists visit (mainly international) during the week. The ratio of national to international visitors is estimated at about four or five to one.

No overall visitation statistics have been kept recently at Izta-Popo Park. Statistics were kept between 1967 and 1975, during which time the park received over 1,000,000 visitors, ranking as the ninth most-visited national park. At the present time, the numbers of overnight visitors are recorded at the lodge, which is the only source of statistical information.

From 1984 through 1987 (see Table 1, previously presented), 13,902 foreign visitors registered at the Vicente Guerrero Mountain Lodge. Of these, 48.5 percent or 6,757, came from the United States; 2,105 or 15.1 percent from West Germany; 5.8 percent or about 800 from Canada, France, and Switzerland; 1.3 percent from the United Kingdom; and 1 percent from Austria. The predominance of North Americans is explained by the fact that they represent over 90 percent of international tourism to Mexico. In addition, several American mountaineering clubs (i.e., Mountain Travel, American Alpine Institute) based on the West Coast offer 3 to 4-day mountaineering tours to the park. Most of the visitors come to the park for mountaineering, trekking, and climbing.

C. WWF Park Survey Results

1. Visitor Profile

Specific data on visitor patterns and profiles were obtained by WWF during two survey weeks,[1] when 90 international and 284 national visitors were interviewed.[2]

a) National Visitors

Most national visitors come from nearby Mexico City (73 percent) or Puebla (10 percent). The majority of visitors were male (67 percent) and had a mean age of 29.5. Visitors were accompanied by relatives (50 percent) or by friends and colleagues (43 percent). Eleven percent indicated that they were traveling with a tour group.

Main motivation for visiting Izta-Popo was clearly recreation (57 percent), the short trip (27 percent), adventure (13 percent), geology (13 percent), and the park's fauna (10 percent).

Nature-related activities by national visitors included hiking and trekking, mountaineering, wildlife observation, botany and birdwatching.

---

[1]One week in high season (February), and one week in low season May).

[2]A random sample of 41 international and 30 national visitors was selected for the purpose of data analysis.

Visitors generally arrive by automobile (90 percent). A much smaller group travels by bus (10 percent). The mean number of nights national tourists spent in or near the park was 3.2, almost half of them indicating that they stayed overnight at the lodge or at a camping site. Over 75 percent stated that they had visited Izta-Popo before, the mean number of previously reported visits being 5.9.

b) International Tourists

The nationality distribution of the survey participants is similar to that of guests at Guerrero Mountain Lodge, with North Americans constituting about 50 percent of all international tourists visiting Izta-Popo, while the share of Europeans with over 43 percent is relatively high. Two-thirds of all international visitors were male, having a mean age of 32 and a mean annual income between U.S. $20,000 and U.S. $29,999. Tourists were mostly accompanied by friends and colleagues (48 percent), by relatives (18 percent), or came alone (18 percent).

Almost two-thirds had planned their excursion to Izta-Popo before traveling to Mexico. The remainder spontaneously visited the Park based upon recommendations from friends, brochures, and other local souces. A majority of visitors used automobiles (68 percent) or buses (30 percent) to get to the park. The mean number of nights spent in or near the park was 3.4 nights, only slightly more than national visitors. Almost 60 percent indicated that they had stayed at the lodge or camped while visiting the park, while 18 percent used a pension.

The main motivations for visiting Izta-Popo were given as its geology (55 percent), and adventure (55 percent), recreation (30 percent), the shortness of the trip from Mexico City (25 percent), and the flora (21 percent).

Nature-related activities performed by international tourists while visiting the park included mountaineering (74 percent), hiking (66 percent), botany (23 percent), and birdwatching (9 percent).

2. Visitor Impressions

Also obtained from the WWF park surveys were visitors' impressions of the park as a tourist attraction.

a) National Visitors

All national visitors evaluated their experience visiting Izta-Popo as excellent (54 percent) or good (46 percent). The park's infrastructure and installations also received high marks, being rated as good (61 percent) or excellent (39 percent).

National visitors enjoyed the park's natural features, the lodge, the flora, and the climate but criticized the extent of pollution and litter, the lack of wildlife and environmental protection, and the unavailability of transport to and from the park.

Recommended improvements included provision of guide books and technical information, park cleanup, control of litter and pollution, distribution of pamphlets at the park entrance, discussion about the park and park regulations, and improvement of the road system.

Future problems as perceived by national visitors are deforestation and lack of funding to maintain the park.

b) International Visitors

Most international visitors found their experience visiting Izta-Popo as excellent (69 percent) or good (26 percent) and expressed satisfaction with the park's infrastructure, classifying it as excellent (46 percemt) or good (46 percent), while some criticized installations as mediocre (5 percent) or poor (2 percent).

International visitors enjoyed the park's natural features, the lodge, the people, and the flora, but indicated as the dislikes, pollution and litter, dirty toilet facilities, and lack of nature trail signs and markers.

Asked for ways to improve the parks as a tourist attraction, visitors recommended improved guide books, technical information in various languages, maps, improved transportation to and from the park, and an increase in the number of nature trails.

Future problems of the park as perceived by international tourists included increased effects of tourism on wildlife and the environment, pollution and litter, erosion, overuse of the area, ecological destruction, and lack of respect for the park on the part of nationals.

D. Economic Impacts of Tourism to Izta-Popo

There is no entrance fee to Izta-Popo, but there is a minimal entrance fee (under U.S. $1) at the lodge for overnight visitors. The main economic activity in the park is the restaurant inside the lodge, which has a seating capacity of 150.

The restaurant employs nine people during the week and 15 on the weekends. It is concessioned from the park, and therefore, the owner pays rent to the park.

Also in the lodge, there is a small area where post cards, pins, and posters are sold. Mountain climbing gear can also be rented for a minimal price.

SEDUE employs about 35 people to maintain the park. This includes a park manager, technical advisor, park guards, and people to work at the lodge and in the laundry.

Other economic activities related to the tourism at Izta-Popo can be seen outside the park. Just before the park entrance, there are several stands where foods and beverages are sold. There is also some economic impact is the closest town, Amecameca, which is 22 kilometers from Izta-Popo. Some park visitors spend the night there. A more significant impact is the number of local taxis that are hired at the bus terminal in Amecameca to take visitors to the mountains.

E. Environmental Impacts of Tourism to Izta-Popo

Some negative environmental impacts have been noticed at the park. Although fairly minor at present, they could easily get out of control. There is an increasing amount of garbage in the area. Some tourists cut live trees for their campfires, which leads to deforestation and also to the potential for forest fires. Another environmental problem from tourism is an increase of refuse that is not being adequately treated. Solid garbage at the lodge is thrown away at some distance from the lodge, and wastewater is being discharged into a nearby gully. This is degrading the water quality of the spring 5.4 kilometers below the lodge.

VI. Cañon del Sumidero National Park (Case Study #2)

A. General Description and Infrastructure

The Sumidero Canyon is one of the most spectacular geological faults in the Americas. The gigantic chasm was formed some 12 million years ago and its walls, almost vertical, plunge more than 1,300 meters to its inner gorge, where the Grijalva River, dammed in 1980, flows towards the Gulf of Mexico. Around the rim, vegetation is composed of dry tropical deciduous forest and on the lower slopes of the gorge and the riverside, there are pockets of a more humid, denser, evergreen forest.

The wildlife of Sumidero is abundant, including such species as crocodiles, white-tailed deer, spider monkey, anteater, and many birds, such as the great curassow, red-breasted chat, flammulated flycatcher, and belted flycatcher. Geographically, the area represents the meeting place of the Gulf coast and Pacific coast avifauna and is thus particularly important to and highly popular with American birdwatchers.

The park's infrastructure is scarce, limited to a highway bordering the western rim of the canyon, five lookout points with some picnic facilities, and two restaurants operated by concession. There is also a concessioned boat service for visiting the Sumidero by river; the boat concession has two docks for boarding, one in Cahuaré and the other in the picturesque town of Chiapa de Corzo.

The park, which is located near the city of Tuxtla Gutiérrez, the capital of the state of Chiapas, can be accessed by two different modes and entrances. Visitors enter by a paved road from Tuxtla Gutiérrez or by boat down the Grijalva River.

B. Visitor Information to Date

Sumidero National Park is one of the few national parks in Mexico where visitation statistics have been kept regularly and systematically over the last five years, according to SEDUE records. As may be seen in Table 2, presented previously, a total of 477,684 people visited the park during the period 1983-1987. Of this total, 425,975 or 89.5 percent were national visitors, and 49,709 or 10.5 percent were international visitors. Tourism has steadily increased over these years, as illustrated in the drammatic rise of 22.4 percent from 1986 to 1987.

Peak months of visitation at Sumidero are (from highest to lowest): August, July, April, December, January, and March. Months with the lowest number of visitors (starting with the lowest figure) are: June, May, February, September, October, and

November. This means that three high-season periods can be detected: school vacations in summer, Easter or spring vacations, and escape from the colder winter months further north.

The number of foreign visitors to Sumidero has been increasing, with a 78.7 percent increase from 1983 to 1987. This increase is also reflected proportionally, since foreign visitors constituted only 6.7 percent of total visitors in 1983, but over 14.8 percent in 1987. High season for foreign visitors is October - April; July and August also show high seasonality. Peak months for national visitors appear to be July, August, April, and December.

No annual breakdowns showing nationalities, sex, or adult/child distribution for foreign visitors were available, but representative statistics for the month of December 1987 reveal the distribution shown in Table 3. During this month, a total of 9,321 people visiting the park by land were registered, of which 607 were foreigners and 8,714 Mexican. Foreign visitors came from the following countries: U.S.: 169 (27.8 percent of all foreigners), West Germany: 120 (19.8 percent), Guatemala: 99 (16.3 percent), France: 72 (11.9 percent), Italy: 31 (5.1 percent), Switzerland, Canada, and El Salvador each 20 (3.3 percent), and United Kingdom: 9 (1.5 percent). Of these totals, 304 were adult males, 254 adult females, and 49 children.

During that same period, 8,714 nationals (93.5 percent of total visitors) visited the park. Most came from the same state of Chiapas (46.2 percent), México (including presumably Mexico City - 24.5 percent), Veracruz (6.2 percent), Oaxaca (5.8 percent), Tabasco (4.1 percent), Jalisco (2.4 percent), Morelos (2.1 percent), and Nuevo Leon (2 percent). Veracruz, Oaxaca, and Tabasco are adjacent states. A majority of the national visitors (3,766) were adult men; 3,411 were adult women; and 1,537 were children. All visitors for the month of December used a total of 33 buses and 1,693 automobiles to visit the park.

Table 3.

MONTHLY VISITOR DISTRIBUTION
SUMIDERO NATIONAL PARK
1983 - 1987

MONTH	TOTAL	NATIONALS	%	FOREIGN	%
January	36,011	32,016	88.9	3,995	11.1
February	28,424	24,471	86.1	3,953	13.9
March	33,847	29,730	87.8	4,117	12.2
April	54,658	48,437	88.6	6,221	11.4
May	28,485	26,570	93.3	1,915	6.7
June	27,776	26,115	94.0	1,661	6.0
July	61,126	57,110	93.4	4,016	6.6
August	63,329	55,972	88.4	7,357	11.6
September	28,822	26,265	91.1	2,557	8.9
October	29,023	24,520	84.5	4,920	15.5
November	31,661	26,741	84.5	4,920	15.5
December	52,522	48,028	91.4	4,494	8.6
Total	477,684	425,975	89.5	49,709	10.5

Source: SEDUE, Chiapas

The park is visited mostly by week-end excursionists. The percentage of foreign tourists coming to the park solely for natural exploration (primarily birdwatching) is estimated at 5 percent by the park manager.

C. WWF Park Survey Results

1. Visitor Profile

Data on visitor patterns and profiles were obtained during two survey weeks,[3] when 81 international and 297 national visitors[4] were interviewed.

---

[3] One week in March (high season), and one week in May (low season).

[4] For the data analysis, a random sample of 30 national visitors and 40 international visitors was selected.

134

a) National Visitors

National visitors were predominantly male (73 percent), and the mean age was 32.7. Visitors tended to be in groups of relatives (47 percent) or friends and colleagues (37 percent). Only 7 percent came with a tour group. Transportation to reach the park was provided mostly by automobiles (80 percent) and buses (23 percent). National visitors spent a mean number of 1.4 nights in or near the park, using good quality hotels (17 percent), lodges or camps (10 percent) or private homes (13 percent). Over 57 percent had visited the park before, averaging 9.7 previous visits.

Major motivations for visiting Sumidero were recreational (53 percent). Other reasons included the park's geology (43 percent), adventure (20 percent), fauna (20 percent), and short trip length (17 percent).

Nature-related activities performed by national visitors included wildlife observation, boat excursion, birdwatching, and botany.

b) International Visitors

Europeans accounted for a surprising 65 percent of all international visitors, almost half from France. North Americans constituted only 30 percent of park visitors. Park personnel claim that the park normally receives a large proportion of German visitors, though this was not the case when WWF surveys were conducted.

Almost two-thirds of international visitors were male, and visitors had a mean age of 47.4. International visitors generally came in a tour group (55 percent) or were accompanied by relatives (28 percent) or friends and colleagues (25 percent).

Motivations for visiting the Sumidero included its geology (45 percent), short trip length (30 percent), its fauna (30 percent), recreation (20 percent), rare species (15 percent) and adventure (13 percent). Nature-related activities engaged in by international park visitors were birdwatching, boat excursions, botany, wildlife observation, and jungle excursions.

Fifty-eight percent of international visitors used automobiles to reach the park, 43 percent took a bus, and 20 percent traveled by plane. International visitors stayed slightly longer in or near the park than national visitors, remaining a mean number of 1.4 nights, mainly using good quality local hotels (55 percent). Over 66 percent had planned to visit Sumidero before arriving in Mexico, while the remainder decided to visit the park based upon recommendations from friends or guides or other local advice.

2. Visitor Impressions

Visitors' impressions of Sumidero as a tourist destination were also obtained from the WWF park surveys.

a) National Visitors

National visitors considered their park experience to be either excellent (63 percent) or good (33 percent). The park's infrastructure was rated predominantly as good (by 59 percent) or excellent (by 35 percent). Seven percent classified the park infrastructure as poor.

National visitors enjoyed the park's natural features and resources, the look-outs, the flora, and the park guards, but they criticized damaged facilities, lack of plant and wildlife checklists and technical information on the area, pollution and litter, and lack of wildlife and environmental protection.

To improve the park as a tourist attraction, national visitors recommended improving guidebooks, technical information, overlooks, and transportation, cleaning up and controlling litter, and improving the park's infrastructure.

Future problems the park might face, according to some of the nationals interviewed, are ecological destruction, lack of respect for natural resources of the park on behalf of the local population, and maintaining the facilities.

b) International Visitors

International visitors evaluated their experience in the park predominantly as good (56 percent) or excellent (42 percent). Although a majority rated the park's infrastructure as either good (56 percent) or excellent (19 percent), more than 22 percent gave infrastructure a mediocre rating.

International visitors enjoyed the park's natural features and resources, birdwatching, the local flora, and the restaurant, but some criticized the lack of available technical information and checklists on the area, the lack of nature trails, and the condition of the roads.

Asked for ways how to improve the park as a tourist destination, international tourists recommended improving guidebooks, providing maps and technical information, installing concessions, and improving tourist services.

Future problems as perceived by some of the international visitors included deforestation, increased effects of tourism on

wildlife and environment, and environmental problems caused by
motor boats.

D. Economic Impacts of Tourism to Sumidero

As in other national parks, no entrance fee is charged at
Sumidero. Fourteen park guards and a park manager are employed
by SEDUE to maintain the area. There are no economic activities
on the park grounds that contribute to the park budget.

Three tourist services operate inside the park, although
none of them is concessioned to the park. Income is gained
through a restaurant at the Los Chiapas Lookout, which is
concessioned to the state government; income also comes from a
newer restaurant on the riverside, owned and operated by workers
of the Comision Federal de Electricidad, and from a tourist boat
service.

Some economic impact from tourism to Sumidero is experienced
in the nearby city of Tuxtla Gutiérrez, although this is
difficult to quantify. Tuxtla Gutiérrez receives a great number
of visitors, but how many of them have been to Sumidero has not
been calculated. Many travel and tour agencies opoerate in
Tuxtla, and some of them offer trips to Sumidero.

E. Environmental Impacts of Tourism to Sumidero

Negative environmental impacts at Sumidero thus far have
been limited. They include forest fires, some of which are
caused by tourists. Fires are most frequent during the peak of
the dry season, from March to May, and have been causing serious
damage to large patches of local flora in the park.   Water
pollution and litter are other problems that have been associated
with tourists.   A positive side of these problems is that
park guards are realizing that detrimental effects are occurring
on the resources and consequently, on the tourism industry, and
the guards are beginning to put pressure on SEDUE to increase
park maintenance.

APPENDIX A

REVIEW OF NATURE TOURISM LITERATURE

Alcérreca, Carlos. 1988. <u>Fauna Silvestre y Areas Naturales Protegidas</u>, Fundación Universo Veintiuno, A.C.

Allen, R. 1980. How to Save the World Strategy for World Conservation. Routledge & Kegan Paul, London.

Almagor, Uri. 1985. "A Tourist's 'Vision Quest' in an African Game Reserve," Annals of Tourism Research 12 (1):31-47.

Alpine, Lisa. 1986. "Trends in Special Interest Travel," in Speciality Travel Index 13:83-84.

Anders, Cindy. 1988. "Who's Watching the Parks?," in Mexico Journal 27: 16-22.

Ashbaugh, Byron L. 1963. Planning a Nature Center. National Audubon Society. New York City, New York.

Ashbaugh, Byron L. and Raymond J. Kordish. 1965. Trail Planning and Layout. National Audubon Society. New York City, New York.

Bachman, Earl E. 1967. Recreation Facilities. Forest Service, US Department of Agriculture. Pacific Southwest Forest and Range Experiment Station, Berkeley, California.

Bachman, Philipp. 1987. <u>Tourism in Kenya: A Basic Need for Whom?</u> Berne, Lang Publishers.

Bacon, Peter R. 1987. "Use of Wetlands for Tourism in the Insular Caribbean," in Annals of Tourism Research, Vol. 14 pp.104-117,

Barrett, Mary Ellin. 1987. "Vacationers Hear the Call of the Wild," in USA Today, December 1.

Bjonness, Inger-Mari. 1980. "Ecological Conflicts and Economic Dependency on Tourist Trekking in Sagarmatha (Mt. Everest) National Park, Nepal. An Alternative Approach to Park Planning," in Norsk Geografische Tidsskrift 3/80.

BNTMP. 1988. Belize National Tourism Marketing Programme. Belmopan, Belize.

Boullon, Roberto C. 1985. Planificacion del Espacio Turistico. Editorial Trillas, Mexico.

Boza, Mario A. 1986. <u>Parques Nacionales Costa Rica National Parks</u>. Fundación de Parques Nacionales, Costa Rica.

Budowski, Gerardo. 1973. "Tourism and the Conservation of Nature: Conflict, Coexistence or Symbiosis," key note address, Kyoto, Japan, February 22-23.

Budowski, Gerardo. 1977. "Tourism and Conservation: Conflict, Coexistence, or Symbiosis?," in Parks 1(4).

Caribbean Development Bank. 1982. Tourism Development Strategy. Summary and Statement.

Castillo, Roberto and J. Gutierrez Roa. 1981. "El Geografo en al Evaluacion de los Recursos Naturales Turisticos," Memoria VII Congreso Nacional de Geografia. SMGE. Mexico.

Ceballos-Lascurain, Hector. 1976 Informacion Preliminar sobre el Parque Natural de la Ballena Gris en Baja California. INDECO, Mexico.

Ceballos-Lascurain, Hector. 1984. "Ecotechniques Applied to Urban Development and Housing: SEDUE's ECODUVI Project," in Proceedings of the International Conference on Passive and Low Energy Ecotechniques held in Mexico City, August 6-11. Pergamon Press, Mexico.

Ceballos-Lascurain, Hector. 1987. "Estudio de Prefactibilidad Socioeconomica del Turismo Ecologico y Anteproyecto Arquitectonico y Urbanistico del Centro de Turismo Ecologico de Sian Ka'an, Quintana Roo," study made for SEDUE, Mexico.

Ceballos-Lascurain, Hector. 1988. "The Future of Ecotourism," Mexico Journal: January 17: 13-14.

Ceballos-Lascurain, Hector. 1988. Tourism Report I, II, to World Wildlife Fund.

Centro Agronomico Tropical de Investigacion y Ensenanza (CATIE). 1980. Parque Nacional Volcan Poas: Plan Para el Desarrollo del Programa Interpretativo. Turrialba, Costa Rica.

Chaverri, Robert. 1988. "Programa de Accion Inmediata para el Mejoramiento de la Oferta Turistica". Instituto Costarricense de Turismo.

Chesire, Ben. 1985. "Nepal Learns to Live with the Fruits of Tourism," in Contours 2(2):6-10.

Cifuentes Arias, Miguel. 1984. Plan de Manejo y Desarrollo, II

Fase; Parque National Galápagos. Comisión de alto nivel Plan Maestro de Galápagos, Grupo Técnico, Quito.

Cloud, John. 1985. "Forest Resources and Rural Populations in Chiapas," in Cultural Survival 9(1), pp.21-24.

Coburn, Robert. 1979. "Sagarmatha: Managing a Himalayan World Heritage Site," in Parks 9(2):10-13.

Coe, Edward M. and Chuck Y. Gee. 1986. Plan Estratégico De Comercialización del Turismo en el Ecuador. Private Sector Initiatives Project, Agency for International Development (AID).

Cohen, Erik. 1978. "The Impact of Tourism on the Physical Environment," in Annals of Tourism Research, Vol. 5(2), pp. 215-229.

Cristiansen, Monty L. 1977. Park Planning Handbook. Fundamentals of Physical Planning for Parks and Recreation Areas. John Wiley and Sons, New York.

CTRC. 1985. Tourism Action Plan for Belize. Caribbean Tourism Research and Development Centre (CTRC), Barbados.

CTRC. 1986a. Dominica. Visitor Expenditure and Motivation Survey. Caribbean Tourism and Development Research Centre, Barbados.

CTRC. 1986b. An Overview of Tourism as a Major Positive Force in Caribbean Economic Growth and Development. Caribbean Tourism Research and Development Centre, Barbados.

CTRC. 1987a. Visitor Spending in the Caribbean 1986. Caribbean Tourism Research and Development Center, Barbados.

CTRC. 1987b. The Contribution of Tourism to Economic Growth and Development in the Caribbean. Caribbean Tourism Research and Development Center, Barbados.

Dameyer, Christina. 1986. "Pakistan Aims at the Adventure Market: Conference Confirms Country's Potential," in Pacific Travel News 30 (7):15-16.

D'Amore, Louis J. 1988. "Tourism - The World's Peace Industry", in Business Quarterly. School of Business Administration, The University of Western Ontario/London.

Dasmann, Raymond F., John P. Miller and Peter H. Freeman. 1973. Ecological Principles for Economic Development. John Wiley and Sons, Ltd. New York.

de Alba Perez, Carlos R. 1980. "Consideraciones sobre el Impacto de las Actividades Humanas en las Poblaciones de Aves y Mamíferos

Marinos en Baja California Sur," in Proceedings of Seminario 80 Baja California Sur sobre la Conservacion del Ambiente en Sitios Turisticos. Secretaria de Turismo, Mexico.

de Groot, R.S. 1983. "Tourism and Conservation in the Galapagos Islands," in Biological Conservation 26(4):291-300.

Delgado, Jesus M. 1986. "Perspectivas Economicas de los Parques Nacionales Venezolanos," 27a sesion de trabajo de la comision de parques nacionales y areas protegidas, Bariloche, Argentina, March.

Devas, Esmond. 1980. Visitor Expenditure in Dominica. WTO/CTRC.

DITURIS. 1986. Ecuador. Boletín de Estadísticas Turísticas. Quito, Ecuador.

DITURIS. 1988. Boletin de Estadisticas Turisticas. 1988. Quito, Ecuador.

Dominica Tourist Board. 1987. "Tourism - A Country Profile," prepared for the Commonwealth Small States Exposition, Vancouver-Toronto, October 11-25.

Durst, Patrick B. and C. Denise Ingram. 1987. "How Well Do Developing Countries Promote Nature-Oriented Tourism by Mail?," in FPEI Working Paper No. 25, Raleigh, North Carolina.

Dwyer, J.F. and M.D. Bowes. 1979. "Benefit-Cost Analysis for Appraisal of Recreation Alternatives, in J. Forest 77(3):445-8.

Economic Research Associates. 1985. Desarrollo Turistico: Canales de Tortuguero. Reporte Final.

The Economist. 1987. "International Tourism Reports". No.1, National Report No.129. The Economist Publications Ltd.

The Economist. 1987. "International Tourism Reports". No.3, National Report No.140. The Economist Publications Ltd.

Edington, John and Ann. 1986. Ecology, Recreation and Tourism. Cambridge University Press. Cambridge, England.

Edwards, Marie-José. 1988. Report on Tourism in Dominica.

Ehrlich, H. and M.A. Vaccaro. 1972. "Disney's New World," in Asia Magazine, December 24, pp. 3-12.

Emory, Jerry. 1988. "Managing Another Galapagos Species - Man," National Geographic Magazine 173(1): 146-154.

Estrategia Nacional de Conservacion. 1976

Evans, Peter G.H. 1986. "Dominica, West Indies," in World Birdwatch, Vol. 8(1).

Fagrell, Truls. 1988. "Spectacular Nature Tours to Mexico Attracting Governments Attention," Travel Mexico, Mexico.

Ferrario, Franco F. 1980. "Tourist Potential and Resource Assessment," in Hawkins, Donald e. et al (ed). Tourism Planning and Development issues. George Washington University. Washignton, D.C. pp. 311-320.

Frechtling, Douglas C. 1987. "Assessing the Impacts of Travel and Tourism - Measuring Economic Benefits," in Richie, J.R.B. and C.R. Goeldner (eds) Travel, Tourism and Hospitality Research - A Handbook for Managers and Researchers, pp. 333-51.

Frueh, Susanne. 1986. Problems in a Tropical Paradise. The Impacts of International Tourism on Cancún, Mexico. Masters Thesis, University of South Carolina, Columbia, S.C.

Frueh, Susanne. 1988. Report to WWF on Tourism to Protected Areas.

Garcés, F., J. Ortiz and C. Vela. 1984. Diagnóstico del la Actividad Turística de la Provincia de Galápagos y sus Impactos Sociales y Ecológicos. INGALA, Pto Ayora, Galápagos.

Garrett, Wilbur E. 1988. "La Ruta Maya: A Proposal," editor, National Geographic Magazine.

General Directorate of Civil Aviation. 1988.

Gonzales, Victor. 1988. Tourism Report I, II, to World Wildlife Fund.

Gorio, Sylvanus. 1978. "Papua New Guinea Involves Its People in National Park Development," in Parks 3(2):12-14.

Greish. 1987. EEC Tourism Advisor.

Gutierrez Roa, Jesus. 1977. Parque Natural Los Azufres, Michoacan. Simposio Mexicano-Polaco Sobre el Aprovechamiento de Recursos Geograficos de America Latina. UAEM. Mexico.

Gutierrez Roa, Jesus. 1983. Excursiones. Editorial Limusa. Mexico.

Gutierrez Roa, Jesus and R. Cstillo G., J. Castaneda G., J.A. Sanchez O. 1986. Recursos Naturales y Turismo. Editorial Limusa. Mexico.

Hartshorn, Gary et al. 1984. <u>Belize Country Environmental Profile: A Field Study</u>. Robert Nicolait & Associates Ltd., Belize City, Belize.

Healy, Robert G. 1988. "Economic Considerations in Nature-Oriented Tourism: The Case of Tropical Forest Tourism". Southeastern Center for Forest Economics Research, Research Triangle Park, NC. FPEI Working Paper No. 39.

Henry, Wesley R. 1979. "Patterns of Tourist Use in Kenya's Amboseli National Park: Implications for Planning and Management," in Hawkins, Donald E., and Elwood, L. Schafer, James M. Rovelstad, eds. Tourism Marketing and Management Issues. Washington, D.C.: George Washington University, pp. 43-57.

Heyman Art. 1988. "Natural Tourism Attractions: It Pays To Protect Them," Organization of American States (OAS), unpublished paper.

Heyman, Arthur. July 22-24, 1987. "Natural Tourism Attractions: Their Preservation and Development," XV Inter-American Travel Congress, OEA/Ser. K. III. 16.1, TURISMO.

Heyman, A, <u>et.al</u>. April 1988. "Project Proposal for the Development of Tobago Cays National Park, St. Vincent and the Grenadines," Organization of American States, Washington, D.C.

Hough, John. 1987. "New Directions for Parks? Issues from the 20th International Parks Seminar," Parks 12(2):9-11.

Houseal, Brian, Craig MacFarland, Guillermo Archibold, Aurelio Chiari, 1985. "Indigenous Cultures and Protected Areas in Central America," in Cultural Survival Vol 9,1(2).

Ingram, C. Denise and Patrick B. Durst, 1987. "Nature-Oriented Travel to Developing Countries," FPEI Working Papers Series No. 28, Raleigh, North Carolina.

Instituto Nacional de Investigaciones Forestales. 1979. Memoria del III Simposio Binacional Sobre el Medio Ambiente del Golfo de California. Eocodesarrollo. Publicacion Especial INIF No 14. Mexico.

International Union for the Conservation of Nature and Natural Resources (IUCN). 1985. "Threatened Natural Areas, Plants and Animals of the World," Parks 10(1):15-17.

Jeffries, Bruce E. 1982. "Sagarmatha National Park: The Impact of Tourism in the Himalayas," in Ambio 11(5):274-281.

Krutilla, J.V. (ed) 1972. Natural Environment. John Hopkins University Press, Baltimore.

Kumpumula, M. 1979. The Influence Of Visitor's On The Predators Of Amboseli National Park. Masters Thesis, University of Nairobi, Nairobi, Kenya.

Kutay, Kurt. 1989. "Ecotourism - Making Peace with Nature and Humanity, in Buzzworm: The Environmental Journal.

Laarman, Jan G. 1987. "Nature-Oriented Tourism in Costa Rica and Ecuador" Diagonosis of Research Needs and Project Opportunities," in FPEI Working Paper No. 6, Raleigh, North Carolina.
Laarman, Jan G. and Richard R. Perdue, 1987a. "A Survey of Return Visits to Costa Rica By OTS Participants and Associates," in FPEI Working Paper No. 29, Raleigh, North Carolina.

Laarman, Jan G. and Richard R. Perdue, 1987b. "Tropical Tourism as Economic Activity: OTS in Costa Rica," in FPEI Working Paper No. 33.

Laarman, Jan G. and Patrick B. Durst, 1987. "Nature Travel in the Tropics. Is this Growing Enterprise a Trend in Wildlands Management?," in Journal of Forestry, Vol. 85, No. 5.

Lewin, R. 1978. "Galapagos: The Rise of Optimism," in New Scientist 79(1113):261-263.

Ley General del Equilibrio Ecologico y la Proteccion al Ambiente. 1988. Secretaria de Desarrollo Urbano y Ecologia.

Lopez Ornat, Arturo and J.J. Consejo. 1986. Plan de Manego de la Reserva de la Biosfera Sian Ka'an. Direccion de Conservacion Ecologica de los Recursos Naturales. SEDUE. Mexico.

Machlis, Gary E. and R.P. Neumann. 1987. The State of National Parks in the Neotropical Realm. Parks 12(2): 3-8.

MacKinnon, John and Kathy et al (compiler). 1986. Managing Protected Areas in the Tropics. IUCN, Gland, Switzerland.

McHarg, Ian L. 1969. Design with Nature. Doubleday & Company, Inc. Garden City, New York.

Manly, Richard J. (ed). 1977. Guidelines for Interpretive Building Design. National Audubon Society. New York.

Manning, Robert E. 1980. "International Aspects of National Park Systems: Focus on Tourism," in Hawkins, Donald E., and Elwood L.

Shafer, James M. Rovelstad, eds. Tourism Planning and Development Issues. Washington, D.C.: George Washington University, pp. 179-192.

Marcondes, M.A.P. 1981. Aptación de una Metodología de Evaluación Económica, Aplicada al Parque Nacional Cahuita, Costa Rica. Centro Agronómico Tropical de Investigación y Enseñanza, Serie Técnica no. 19.

Mathieson, Allister and Geoffrey Wall. 1982. <u>Tourism: Economic, Physical, and Social Impacts</u>. London, Longman.

Matthews, D.O. 1962. "The Economics of Parks and Tourism," in Adams, A.B., ed. Proceedings, First World Conference on National Parks. June 30-July 7; East Africa Tourist Travel Association, pp. 113-124.

McMurtry, Ruth M. 1986. Design for Ecotourism in the Caribbean Tropics: Bibliography. School of Architecture & Urban Planning. University of Wisconsin, Milwaukee, Wisconsin.
McNeely, Jeffrey A. and Kenton R. Miller. 1984. "National Parks, Conservation and Development. The Role of Protected Areas in Sustaining Society," proceedings of the World Congress on National Parks, Bali, Indonesia, October 11-22, 1982. Smithsonian Institution Press, Washington, D.C.

McNeely and Thorsell. 1987. Guidelines for Development of Terrestrial and Marine National Parks for Tourism and Travel. IUCN. Gland, Switzerland.

McNulty, Robert H. 1986. "Cultural Tourism: Wedding Conservation to Economic Development," in Place. July-August.
Miller, Kenton R. 1980. Planificacion de Parques Nacionales para el Ecodesarrollo en el Latinoamerica. Fundacion para la Ecologia y la Proteccion del Medio Ambiente. Madrid.

Miller, Luther Gordon. 1982. Visitor Expenditure in Dominica.

Miller, Luther Gordon. 1988. "The Development of a Tourism Sector Policy for Belize", paper presented at a meeting of The Belize Embassy's Inter-Agency Contact Group, Washington, DC, May 20.

Misrah, Hemantha R. 1982. "A Delicate Balance: Tigers, Rhinoceros, Tourists and Park Management Vs. the Needs of the Local People in Royal Chitwan National Park, Nepal," in McNeely, Jeffrey A.; Miller, Kenton, eds. Proceedings, World Congress on Protected Areas; 1982 October 11-22, Bali, Indonesia, pp. 197-205.

Mittermeier, R. 1986. "Conservation Action in the Megadiversity Countries," paper presented at the National Forum on

Biodiversity. Smithsonian Intitution, Washington, D.C. Sept.21-24.

Moline, Sergio. 1982. Turismo y Ecología. Editorial Trillas. Mexico.

Monfort, Alain, and Nicole Monfort. 1984. "Akagera: Rwanda's Largest National Park," in Parks 8 (4):6-8.

Moore, Alan. 1980. Análisis de Estadísticas sobre visitas al Parque Nacional Galápagos durante el período comprendido entre Octurbre 1979 y Septiembre 1980; su aplicación al Impacto Turístico. Servicio Parque Nacional Galápagos, Pto. Ayora.

Moore, Alan. 1981a. Análisis de la capacidad de manejo turístico del Servicio Parque Nacional Galápagos. Informe Técnico, SPNG.

Moore, Alan. 1981b. "Tour Guides as a Factor in National Park Management," in Parks, Vol.6,1.

Moore, Alan. 1987. Diagnostico de la Situación del Turismo en Areas del Parque Nacional Galapagos y su Proyección al Futuro. Quito, Ecuador.

Moulin, Claude. 1980. "Plan for Ecological and Cultural Tourism Involving Participation of Local Population and Associations," in Hawkins, Donald E., Schafer, and Elwood L. Schafer, James M. Rovelstad, eds. Tourism Planning and Development Issues. Washington, D.C.: George Washington University, pp. 199-212.

Myers, Norman. 1975. "The Tourist as an Agent for Development and Wildlife Conservation: The Case of Kenya," in International Journal of Social Economics 2(1):26-42.

Myers, Norman. 1972. "National Parks in Savannah Africa: Ecological Requirements of Parks Must be Balanced Against Socio-economic Constraints in their Environments," in Science 178(4067):1255-1263.

Naqshband, Ghulam 1980. "Integration of Tourism and Environment," in Eastern Economist 75(24):1304-1307.

Nordin, Musa Bin. 1976. "Walking Trails in Taman Negara," in Malayan Nature Journal 29(4):242-245.

O'Callaghan, P., J. Woodley, K. Aiken. April 1988. "Project Proposal for the Development of Montego Bay National Park, Jamaica," Organization of American states, Washington, D.C.

O'Connell, P.F. 1977. "Economic Evaluation of Non-Market Goods and Services," in Outdoor Recreation Advances in Applicaton of

Economic Proceedings of National Symposium. U.S. Forest Service. General Technical Report W.).-2, pp. 82-90.

Okey, Roberta. 1987. "Trekking in Nature's Terrarium. Dominica rolls out the green carpet to the adventurous traveler seeking a special solitude," in Americas, September/October.

Olmsted, Karen. 1985. Survey on Tour Operators Offering Bird Tours in North America, Canada and Mexico. Suttons Bay, Michigan.

Organization of American States (OAS). 1984. Planificacion del Desarrollo Regional Integrado. Washington, D.C.

OAS. 1987. Minimum Conflict: Guidelines for Planning the Use of American Humid Tropic Environments. Washington, D.C.

Pearce, D. 1981. Tourist Development. Longman House, New York.

Posner, B., Cuthbertson, E. Towle E., Reeder, C. 1981. Economic Impact Analysis for the Virgin Island National Park. Island Resources Foundation, St. Thomas, US Virgin Islands.

Putney, Allen D. 1974. "Interpretive Plan Poas Volcano National Park. Technical Working Document No 12. FAO/Peace Corps. San Jose, Costa Rica.

Ramos, Mario A. (compiler). 1987. La Diversidad Biologica en Mexico: Identificacion de Prioridades Nacionales," WWF Working Paper. Jalapa, Mexico.

Reilly, William D. 1987. the New Context for Conservation in Latin America," in Place. March/April.

Rogalewski, Olaf. 1973. "Tourism and the Preservation of the Human Environment," in Protection of Man's natural Environment. Polish Academy of Sciences, Warswaw.

Rovinski, Yanina. 1988. Tourism Report I, II, to World Wildlife Fund.

Saglio, Christian. 1979. "Tourism for Discovery: A Project in Lower Casamance, Senegal," in de Kadt, Emanuel, ed. Tourism: Passport to Development? Washington, D.C.: World Bank, pp. 321-335.

Salazar, A.P., and R.M. Huber. 1982. "Ecuador's Active Conservation Program," in Parks 6(4):7-10.

Salm, Rodney V. and J.R. Clark. 1984. Marine and Coastal Protected Areas: A Guide For Plnners and Managers. IUCN. Gland, Switzerland.

Sayer, Jeffrey A. 1981. "Tourism or Conservation in the National Parks of Benin," in Parks 5(4):13-15.

Secretaria de Desarrollo Urbano y Ecologia (SEDUE). 1983. Sistema Nacional de Areas Naturales Protegidas. Mexico.

SEDUE. 1988. Ley General del Equilibrio Ecologico y la Proteccion al Ambiente. Mexico.

Secretaria de Turismo. 1980. Memoria del Seminario 80 Baja Caifornia Sur Sobre la Conservacion del Ambiente en los Sitios Turisticos. La Paz, BCS, Mexico. May 12-14.

Secretaria de Turism. 1987. Delimitacion, Planeacion y Diseno de una Reserva Marina, un Parque Marino y un Acuario en Bahias de Huatulco, Oaxaca, Mexico.

Servicio de Parques Nacionales (1974). Plan Maestro Para la Proteccion y Uso Parque Nacional Volcan Poas. San Jose, Costa Rica.

Shah, Kagda B. 1983. "Mountain Expeditions," in Proceedings, Third International Tourism and Heritage Conservation Conference; 1983 November 1-4; Katmandu, Nepal, pp. 88-91.

Singh, Tej Vir and Kaur, Jagdish. 1986. "The Paradox of Mountain Tourism: Case References from the Himalaya," in Industry and Environment 9(1):21-26.

Sournia, Gerard. 1986. "Integration of National Parks and Faunal Reserves in the Economy of Developing Countries," in Parks, Vol.11, No. 1.

Stevens, Stan. 1988. "Sacred and Profaned Himalayas," Natural History, January: 27-35.

Swift, Byron. 1988. "Ecological Tourism," IUCN Working Paper, Washington, D.C.

Takahashi, Leslie. 1987. Birding Tourism in the Third World: A Look at the Industry, the Destinations, and the Impacts. Master's project, School of Forestry and Environmental Studies, Duke University.

Thorsell, James W. 1982. "National Parks from the Ground up: Experience from Dominica, West Indies," in McNeely, J. and Miller K., eds Proceedings, World Congress on National Parks and Protected Areas; Bali, Indonesia, pp. 616-620.

Thorsell, James W. 1986. "Managing Protected Areas in the Tropics", IUCN, Gland, Switzerland.

Thresher, Philip. 1981. "The Present Value of an Amboseli Lion," World Animal Review 40: 30-33.

Tisdell, Clem A., 1972. "Provision of Parks and the Preservation of Nature - Some Economic Factors," in Australian Economic Papers 11(19), 154-162.

Tisdell, Clem A., 1983. "An Economist's Critique of the World Conservation Strategy with Examples from the Australian Experience," in Environmental Conservation, 10(1), 43-52.

Tisdell, Clem A., 1984. "Tourism, the Environment, International Trade and Public Economics, in ASEAN-Australia Economic Papers No. 6.

Toledo, Victor M. 1987. "La Diversidad Biologica en Mexico: Criterios para Proteger un Patrimonio," paper presented at the meeting on Conservation of the Biological Diversity of Mexico and Identification of National Priorities (organized by WWF). Jalpa, Mexico, May 27-29.

Torres, Antonio. 1988. Tourism Report I, II, to World Wildlife Fund.

U.S. Agency for International Development. 1984. Belize. Country Environmental Profile. A Field Study.

U.S. Fish and Wildlife Service. 1982. National Survey of Fishing, Hunting and Wildlife-Associated Recreation. US Department of the Interior. Washington, D.C.

van't Hof, Tom. 1986. "The Economic Benefits of Marine Parks and Protected Areas in the Caribbean Region," paper prepared for the Sancturary Programs Division, State Department of Commerce, Washington, D.C. 20235.

Vargas Marquez, Fernando. 1984. Parques Nacionales de Mexico. Instituto de Investigaciones Economicas. UNAM. Mexico.

Villa, J.L., and A. Ponce. 1982. "Islands for People and Evolution: The Galapagos," in J.A. McNeely and K.R. Miller (eds.), National Parks, Conservation, and Development, Proceedings of the World Congress on National Parks, Bali, Indonesia, 11-22 October.

Western, David and Phillip Thresher. 1973. Development Plans for Amboseli, Mainly Wildlife Viewing in the Ecosystem. Mimeo, IBRD, Nairobi, Kenya.

Western, David. 1976. "A New Approach to Amboseli" in Parks 1(2):1-4.

Western, David and Wesley R. Henry. 1979. "Economics and Conservation in Third World National Parks," in Bioscience 29(7):414-418.

Western, David. 1982a. "Amboseli," in Swara 5(4):8-14.

Western, David. 1982b. "Amboseli National Park: Human Values and the Conservation of a Savanna Ecosystem," in McNeely, J.A.; and Miller, K.R, eds Proceedings, World Congress on National Parks and Protected Areas; October 11-22, Bali, Indonesia, pp.93-100.

Western, David. 1986. "Tourist Capacity in East African Parks," in Industry and Environment 9(1):14-16.

Williams, Allan M. and Gareth Shaw, eds. 1988. Tourism and Economic Development. London, Pinter Publishers.

Wilson, D. 1979. "The Effects of Tourism in the Seychelles," in Tourism - Passport to Development? ed. E. deKadt, Oxford University Press, New York.

Wilson, Mystie A. 1987a. "Nature-Oriented Tourism in Ecuador: Assessment of Industry Structure and Development Needs," in FPEI Working Paper No. 20, Raleigh, North Carolina.

Wilson, Mystie A. 1987b. "Nature Tourism and Enterprise Development in Ecuador," in FPEI Working Paper No. 27, Raleigh, North Carolina.

Wolbrink, Donald and Associates, Inc. 1973. Physical Standards for Tourism Development. Honolulu: Pacific Islands Development Commission.

World Commission on Environment and Development. 1987. Our Common Future. Oxford University Press. Oxford, New York.

World Tourism Organization. 1983. Tourism's Contribution to Protecting the Environment. WTO. Madrid.

World Tourism Organzation. 1987. Yearbook of Tourism Statistics. Volumes I and II. WTO. Madrid.

Zinder, H. and Associates. 1969. The Future of Tourism in the Eastern Caribbean. Washington, D.C..

APPENDIX B

GLOSSARY OF TERMS

BNTMP: Belize National Tourism Marketing Programme

BTR: Belize Tourism Report

BTIO: Belize Tourism Industry Organization

carrying capacity: the sustainable amount of visitors per day/month/year that and area can support, dependent upon the type or size of protected/natural area, soil, topography, animal behavior, and the number and quality of tourist facilities available

CASEM: Cooperativa de Artesanos de Santa Elena y Monteverde

CATIE: Centro Agrinomico Tropical de Investigacion y Ensenanza

CDP: Community Development Plan

CIPAMEX: The Mexican Section of International Council for Bird Preservation

CTB: Community Tourism Board

CTRC: Caribbean Tourism Research and Development Centre

DITURIS: Direccion Nacional de Turismo de Ecuador

ecological tourism: see nature-oriented tourism

ecotourism: see nature-oriented tourism

EDF: European Development Fund

FONATUR: Fondo Nacional de Fomento al Turismo

GDD: Gross Domestic Product

ICT: Investigacion Costa Ricensa de Turismo

IDB: Inter-American Development Bank

INAINE: Instituto Autonomo de Investigaciones Ecologicas infrastructure -- framework or facilities developed within the protected area for visitor activities, ease of access, and management

IUCN: International Union for the Conservation of Nature and

Natural Resources

leakages: hidden costs which have to be subtracted from the
  gross income derived from tourism

national park: officially designated tract of land

nature tourism: see nature-oriented tourism

nature-oriented tourism: tourism to relatively undisturbed
  natural areas with the specific objective of admiring,
studying and enjoying the scenery and its flora and fauna

NGO: Non-governmental organizations

NNTB: National Nature Tourism Board

OAS: Organization of American States

OECD: Organization for Economic Cooperation and Development

OTS: Organization for Tropical Studies

protected area: officially designated tract of land for the
  preservation of one or more of its natural resources

SECTUR: Secretaria de Turismo

SEDUE: Secretaria de Desarrollo Urbano y Ecologia

SINAP: Sistema Nacional de Areas Naturales Protegidas

SIS: Social Impact Strategy

socio-cultural impacts: impacts from tourism on the community
  and its culture

UNAM: Ecology of the National Autonomous University of Mexico

UNEP: United Nations Environment Programme

UNDP: United Nations Development Programme

USAID: United Stated Agency for International Development

VINP: Virgin Island National Park

WTO: World Tourism Organization

WWF: World Wildlife Fund

APPENDIX C:

WWF Surveys

Fecha:
Aeropuerto:
#

WWF

World Wildlife Fund

ENCUESTA SOBRE TURISMO INTERNACIONAL

El Fondo Mundial para la Naturaleza (WWF) está llevando a cabo un estudio en este país y quisiéramos que usted participara, respondiendo cuidadosamente a este cuestionario. Esa información nos ayudará a determinar el estado de la industria turística en el país y el potencial que existe para turismo a áreas naturales como parques nacionales y reservas. Gracias! Le agradecemos su cooperación!

1. Cuál es su nacionalidad? _____ 2. En qué país vive usted? _____

3. Es usted ( ) HOMBRE o ( ) MUJER (por favor, marque con una X)   EDAD: _____

4. Cuál es su profesión u ocupación? _____

5. Es este su primer viaje a este país?
   1 SI   2 NO (en este caso, cuantas veces ha venido anteriormente?) ____

6. Cuántas noches pasó usted en el país?_____

7. Por qué razón escogió usted este país para este viaje?
   (marque con una X todas las opciones que se apliquen)
   ( ) 1 VISITA A AMIGOS Y/O FAMILIARES   ( ) 2 NEGOCIOS/CONVENCION
   ( ) 3 SOL, PLAYAS, RECREO   ( ) 4 PASEO
   ( ) 5 ARQUEOLOGIA   ( ) 6 HISTORIA CULTURAL
   ( ) 7 HISTORIA NATURAL (botánica, vida silvestre)
   ( ) 8 OTROS (especifique) _____

8. Qué le impulsó a escoger este país como destino de su viaje? (marque todas las opciones que se apliquen)
   ( ) 1 IDEA PROPIA   ( ) 2 RECOMENDACION DE AMIGOS O FAMILIARES
   ( ) 3 PROPAGANDA (especifique_____)
   ( ) 4 DOCUMENTAL EN TELEVISION O REVISTAS (especifique_____
   ( ) 5 OTROS (especifique   )

9. Hasta qué punto influyeron las áreas naturales de este país (como por ejemplo parques nacionales, reservas etc) en su decisión de venir aquí? (una sola opción)
   ( ) 1 MOTIVO PRINCIPAL   ( ) 2 IMPORTANTE, INFLUYO EN MI DECISION
   ( ) 3 RELATIVAMENTE IMPORTANTE ( ) 4 NO TUVO INFLUENCIA EN MI DECISION

10. Quién le acompaña durante este viaje? (por favor, marque con una X)
    ( ) 1 NADIE   ( ) 2 FAMILIARES (especifique el número _____)
    ( ) 3 AMIGOS O COLEGAS
    ( ) 4 GRUPO TURISTICO (especifique el nombre de la compañía) _____
    ( ) 5 OTRO (especifique _____)

11. Qué aerolínea(s) utilizó para su vuelo internacional a y de este país?

12. Favor de calcular de la manera mas aproximada posible la cantidad total que gastó Ud/su familia en su viaje al país, en dólares o en moneda nacional:
    $_____ Moneda nacional _____
    Del total, ____ fueron gastados en pasaje aereo internacional.

1250 Twenty-Fourth Street, NW   Washington, DC 20037   USA   202/293-4800   Telex: 64505 PANDA
Affiliated with The Conservation Foundation

13. Aproximadamente cuanto dinero (en dólares o en moneda nacional) gastó usted/ su familia en los siguientes rubros? (si venía con un paquete, por favor marque con una X los rubros incluídos en el paquete y pone el total)

	dólares	moneda nacional
1 VUELOS INTERNOS		
2 TRANSPORTE INTERNO		
3 ALOJAMIENTO		
4 COMIDAS Y BEBIDAS		
5 GASTOS PERSONALES		
6 TOURS Y EXCURSIONES		
7 SOUVENIRS		
8 OTROS(especifique		

14. Realizó usted alguna de las siguientes actividades relacionadas con la naturaleza durante su visita al país? (marque con una X todas las que se apliquen)
( ) 1 EXCURSIONES A LA SELVA O EL BOSQUE ( ) 2 MONTANISMO
( ) 3 OBSERVACION DE AVES ( ) 4 OBSERVACION DE VIDA SILVESTRE
( ) 5 BOTANICA ( ) 6 PESCA Y CAZA
( ) 7 ACAMPAR ( ) 8 EXCURSIONISMO Y CAMINATAS
( ) 9 VISITA A CULTURAS AUTOCTONAS ( ) 10 PASEOS EN LANCHA O BOTE
( ) 11 OTROS (especifique)

15. Qué areas protegidas/parques nacionales visitó usted ?
_____
_____

16. Qué tipo de alojamiento utilizó usted durante su viaje?
(marque con una X todas las opciones que se apliquen)
( ) 1 HOTEL DE LUJO INTERNACIONAL ( ) 2 HOTEL LOCAL DE BUENA CALIDAD
( ) 3 HOTEL O PENSION SENCILLOS ( ) 4 ALBERGUE DE SELVA/ CAMPAMENTO
( ) 5 BARCO O LANCHA ( ) 6 OTROS (especifique)

17. En general, se considera usted satisfecho(a) por su visita al país?
( ) 1 SI, MUY SATISFECHO(A) ( ) 2 SI
( ) 3 NO MUY IMPRESIONADO(A) ( ) 4 NO, DESILUSIONADO(A)

18. Anote (hasta un total de 4 cosas) lo que mas le gusto de su visita a este pais:
1 _____ 2 _____
3 _____ 4 _____

19. Anote que no le agrado de su visita a este pais
1 _____ 2 _____
3 _____ 4 _____

20. En su opinión, qué podría hacerse para mejorar la calidad de la visita y de la experiencia en el país? Tome en cuenta transporte, logística, guías, información técnica como mapas y guías turísticas, alojamiento, comida?
_____
_____

21. Piensa volver a este pais?
( ) 1 SI ( ) 2 NO

22. Cual es el nivel anual aproximado de ingresos de su familia?
( ) 1 MENOS DE US$ 10,000 ( ) 2 MAS QUE US$ 10,000 ( ) 3 MAS QUE US$ 20,000
( ) 4 MAS QUE US$ 30,000 ( ) 5 MAS QUE US$ 40,000 ( ) 6 MAS QUE US$ 50,000
( ) 7 MAS QUE US$ 100,000
NUEVAMENTE LE AGRADECEMOS SU VALIOSO TIEMPO INVERTIDO A LLENAR ESTE CUESTIONARIO

WWF

World Wildlife Fund

A SURVEY OF INTERNATIONAL TOURISM

The World Wildlife Fund is conducting a tourism study in this country and would like to ask you to participate in this study by answering this questionnaire as accurately as possible. The information will help us assess the country's tourism industry and the potential of tourism to natural sites such as national parks and reserves in the country. We appreciate your cooperation! Thank you!

1. What is your nationality? _____

2. In what country do you live? _____

3. What is your gender? please circle: 1 MALE   2 FEMALE   AGE:____

4.   What is your occupation or profession?   _____

5.   Is this your first trip to this country?
     1   YES
     2   NO (if no, how many times have you been here before? _____)

6.   How many nights did you spend in this country? _____

7.   Why did you choose this country as a travel destination? (circle as many as apply)
     1   VISITING FRIENDS AND/OR RELATIVES   2   BUSINESS/CONVENTION
     3   SUN, BEACHES, ENTERTAINMENT   4   SIGHTSEEING
     5   ARCHAEOLOGY   6   CULTURAL/NATIVE HISTORY
     7   NATURAL HISTORY (i.e. botany, wildlife) 8   OTHER (specify _____)

8.   What influenced you to choose this country as a destination for this trip?
     (circle as many as apply)
     1   OWN IDEA   2   RECOMMENDATION BY FRIENDS OR RELATIVES
     3   ADVERTISEMENTS (specify _____
     4   TV DOCUMENTARIES, MAGAZINES (specify _____
     5   OTHER (specify _____

9.   To what extent did the country's protected areas (i.e. national parks, reserves, etc.)
     influence your decision to come here? (circle one)
     1   MAIN REASON   2   IMPORTANT, INFLUENCED MY COMING HERE
     3   SOMEWHAT IMPORTANT   4   NOT IMPORTANT

10. Who is accompanying you on this trip? (please circle)
     1   NOBODY   2   FAMILY MEMBERS (how many? _____)
     3   FRIENDS AND/OR PROFESSIONAL COLLEAGUES
     4   TOUR GROUP (please name company_____
     5   OTHER (specify _____)

11. What airline(s) did you use for your travel to and from this country?_____

12. Please estimate as best as you can the approximate total amount of money you spent on your
     trip to this country, in US$ or in local currency:
        US$:_____   LOCAL CURRENCY:_____
        of the total, US$ _____ was spent for international airfare

1250 Twenty-Fourth Street, NW   Washington, DC 20037   USA   202/293-4800   Telex: 64505 PANDA
Affiliated with The Conservation Foundation

13. How much money (in US$ or local currency) did you approximately spend on the following
    items? (if you came with a package tour, please circle items included in package)

		US $	LOCAL CURRENCY

    1   AIRPLANE (local travel)   _____
    2   LOCAL TRANSPORTATION   _____
    3   ACCOMODATION   _____
    4   FOOD AND BEVERAGES   _____
    5   PERSONAL EXPENSES   _____
    6   TOURS AND EXCURSIONS   _____
    7   SOUVENIRS   _____
    8   OTHER (specify _____)

14. Did you engage in any of the following nature-related activities while in this country?
    1   JUNGLE EXCURSION   2   MOUNTAIN TREKKING   3   BIRD WATCHING
    4   WILDLIFE WATCHING   5   BOTANY   6   FISHING/HUNTING
    7   CAMPING   8   HIKING   9   VISIT INDIGENOUS CULTURES
    10 BOAT TRIPS   11 OTHER (specify _____)

15. Which protected areas/parks, if any, did you visit? (please list)
    _____
    _____
    _____

16. What type of accomodation did you use during your trip? (circle as many as apply)
    1   HIGH STANDARD INTERNATIONAL HOTEL   2   GOOD QUALITY LOCAL HOTEL
    3   BASIC HOTEL/PENSION   4   JUNGLE LODGE/CAMPING
    5   BOAT/SHIP   6   OTHER (specify _____

17. Overall, were you satisfied with your trip to this country?
    1   YES, EXTREMELY   2   YES
    3   WAS NOT TOO IMPRESSED   4   NO, QUITE DISAPPOINTED

18. Please list up to four things you liked best on your trip to this country:
    1   _____   2   _____
    3   _____   4   _____

19. Please list up to four things you did not like:
    1   _____   2   _____
    3   _____   4   _____

20. In your oppinion, what should be done to improve the quality of the visit and experience?
    Consider transportation, logistics, guide, technical information (i.e. maps, guide books),
    accomodation, food, etc.?
    _____
    _____
    _____

21. Would you consider coming back to this country for another vacation?
    1   YES   2   NO

22. What is the approximate annual income of you and your family?
    1   LESS THAN US$ 10,000   2   OVER US$ 10,000   3   OVER US$ 20,000
    4   OVER US$ 30,000   5   OVER US$ 40,000   6   OVER US$ 50,000
    7   OVER US$ 100,000

ONCE AGAIN, THANK YOU VERY MUCH FOR TAKING THE TIME TO PARTICIPATE IN THIS
QUESTIONNAIRE. IF YOU WANT TO KNOW MORE ABOUT THIS STUDY AND ITS RESULTS
FEEL FREE TO WRITE TO THE WORLD WILDLIFE FUND IN WASHINGTON, D.C., ATTENTION
OF SUSANNE FRUEH, PROJECT DIRECTOR NATURE TOURISM, FOR MORE INFORMATION.

WWF

World Wildlife Fund

CUESTIONARIO SOBRE TURISMO ECOLOGICO

El Fondo Mundial para la Naturaleza (WWF) esta llevando a cabo un estudio en este pais
y quisieramos que usted participara, respondiendo cuidadosamente a este cuestionario.
Esa informacion nos ayudara a determinar el estado de la industria turistica en el
pais y el potencial que existe para turismo a areas naturales como parques nacionales
y reservas. Gracias! Le agradecemos su cooperacion!

1. En que ciudad vive usted? _____

2. Es usted ( ) HOMBRE o ( ) MUJER?   EDAD: _____
   (Por favor, marque con una x)

3. Cuál es su profesión u ocupación? _____

4. Es este su primer viaje a este parque?
   1 SI
   2 NO (en este caso, cuantas veces ha venido anteriormente?) ____

5. Quién le acompaña durante este excursion? (por favor, marque con una X)
   ( ) 1 NADIE   ( ) 2 FAMILIARES (especifique el número _____)
   ( ) 3 AMIGOS O COLEGAS
   ( ) 4 GRUPO TURISTICO (especifique el nombre de la compañía) _____
   ( ) 5 OTRO (especifique _____)

6. Aproximadamente cuánto gastó usted y su familia en los siguientes rubros durante su
excursión a este parque? (si venía con un paquete, marque con una X los rubros
incluidos en el paquete)

                                    DOLARES   MONEDA NACIONAL
   ( ) 1 TRANSPORTE AEREO INTERNO _____
   ( ) 2 TRANSPORTE LOCAL _____
   ( ) 3 GUIA _____
   ( ) 4 ALOJAMIENTO _____
   ( ) 5 COMIDAS Y BEBEIDAS _____
   ( ) 6 GASTOS PERSONALES _____
   ( ) 7 SOUVENIRS _____
   ( ) 8 OTROS (especifique _____

7. Qué tipo de transporte utilizó usted para llegar a este parque? (marque con una X
todas las opciones que se apliquen)
   ( ) 1 AUTOMOVIL   ( ) 2 AUTOBUS
   ( ) 3 AVION   ( ) 4 BARCO O LANCHA
   ( ) 5 OTROS (especifique)

8. Cuantas noches pasó usted en el parque? _____NOCHE(S)

9. Si pasó la noche en el parque, en dónde se alojó?
   ( ) 1 DENTRO DEL PARQUE   ( ) 2 FUERA DEL PARQUE

10. Qué tipo de alojamiento utilizó usted durante todo el viaje a este parque?
( ) 1 HOTEL INTERNACIONAL DE LUJO   ( ) 2 HOTEL LOCAL DE BUENA CALIDAD
( ) 3 PENSION SENCILLA   ( ) 4 CAMPAMENTO
( ) 5 BARCO O LANCHA   ( ) 6 OTROS (especifique)

11. Qué le hizo venir a este parque? (marque todas las opciones que se apliquen)
( ) 1 VIAJE CORTO   ( ) 2 RECREO
( ) 3 AVENTURA   ( ) 4 VIDA SILVESTRE SOBRESALIENTE
( ) 5 FLORA SOBRESALIENTE   ( ) 6 GEOLOGIA Y/O PAISAGE SOBRESALIENTE
( ) 7 ESPECIES RAROS   ( ) 8 OTROS (especifique)_____

12. Cómo calificaría usted su experiencia en este parque?
( ) 1 EXCELENTE   ( ) 2 BUENA
( ) 3 MEDIOCRE   ( ) 4 DECEPCIONANTE

13. Cómo calificaría usted las instalaciones del parque?
( ) 1 EXCELENTES   ( ) 2 BUENAS
( ) 3 MEDIOCRES   ( ) 4 MALAS

14. Qué tipo de actividades relacionadas con la naturaleza ha realizado durante su
visita a este parque?
( ) 1 EXCURSIONES AL BOSQUE O A LA SELVA ( ) 2 MONTANISMO
( ) 3 OBSERVACION DE AVES   ( ) 4 OBSERVACION DE VIDA SILVESTRE
( ) 5 BOTANICA   ( ) 6 PESCA/ CAZA
( ) 7 ACAMPAR   ( ) 8 CAMINATAS O EXCURSIONES
( ) 9 VISITA A CULTURAS AUTOCTONAS ( ) 10 VIAJES EN BOTE
( ) 11 OTROS (especifique)_____

15. Anote (hasta un total de 4 cosas) lo que más le gusto de este parque
1 _____ 2 _____
3 _____ 4 _____

16. Anote (hasta un total de 4 cosas) lo que no le agrado de este parque
1 _____ 2 _____
3 _____ 4 _____

17. En su opinión, qué podría hacerse para mejorar la calidad de la visita y de la
experiencia? Tome en cuenta transporte, logística, guías, información técnica como
mapas y guías turísticas, alojamiento, comida etc.
_____
_____
_____

18. Piensa que este parque tiene o va a tener problemas de cualquier manera?
_____
_____
_____

19. Cual es el nivel anual aproximado de ingresos de su familia?
( ) 1 MENOS DE US$ 5,000   ( ) 2 MAS QUE US$ 5,000
( ) 3 MAS QUE US$ 10,000   ( ) 4 MAS QUE US$ 20,000
( ) 5 MAS QUE US$ 30,000   ( ) 6 MAS QUE US$ 40,000
( ) 7 MAS QUE US$ 50,000   ( ) 8 MAS QUE US$100,000

NUEVAMENTE LE AGRADECEMOS SU VALIOSO TIEMPO INVERTIDO A LLENAR
ESTE CUESTIONARIO.

WWF

World Wildlife Fund

A SURVEY OF INTERNATIONAL NATURE TOURISM

The World Wildlife Fund is conducting a tourism study in this country and would like to ask you to participate in this study by answering this questionnaire as accurately as possible. The information will help us assess the country's tourism industry and the potential tourism to natural sites such as national parks and reserves in the country. We appreciate your cooperation! Thank you!

1. In what city do you live? _____

2. Are you: 1 MALE   2 FEMALE (please circle)   AGE: ____

3. What is your profession/occupation? _____

4. Is this your first excursion to this park?
   1 YES
   2 NO (if no, how many times have you been here before? _____)

5. Who is accompanying you on this trip? (please circle)
   1 NOBODY   2 FAMILY MEMBERS (how many?_____)
   3 FRIENDS AND/OR PROFESSIONAL COLLEAGUES
   4 TOUR GROUP (please name _____)
   5 OTHER (specify _____)

6. During your excursion to this park, how much did you (and your family) approximately spend on the following items? (if you came with a package tour, please circle items included in package and give total)

		US $	LOCAL CURRENCY
1	DOMESTIC AIRFARE		
2	LOCAL TRANSPORTATION		
3	GUIDE		
4	ACCOMODATION		
5	FOOD AND BEVERAGES		
6	PERSONAL EXPENSES		
7	SOUVENIRS		
8	OTHER (specify _____		

7. What type of transportation did you use to come to this park? (circle as many as apply)
   1 CAR   2 BUS   3 AIRPLANE   4 BOAT
   5 OTHER (specify_____)

8. How many nights did you spend in this park? _____NIGHTS

9. If you stayed overnight, where did you stay?
   1 WITHIN THE PARK   2 OUTSIDE THE PARK

10. What type of accomodation did you use during your entire visit to the park?
    1 HIGH STANDARD INTERNATIONAL HOTEL   2 GOOD QUALITY LOCAL HOTEL
    3 BASIC PENSION   4 CAMPING   5 BOAT/SHIP   6 OTHER _____

1250 Twenty-Fourth Street, NW   Washington, DC 20037   USA   202/293-4800   Telex: 64505 PANDA
Affiliated with The Conservation Foundation

11. Why did you come to this park? (circle as many as apply)
    1 SHORT TRAVEL TIME   2 AS DIVERSION FROM CITY/BEACH VACATION
    3 ADVENTURE   4 OUTSTANDING WILDLIFE
    5 OUTSTANDING VEGETATION 6 OUTSTANDING GEOLOGY AND/OR LANDSCAPE
    7 RARE SPECIES   8 OTHER_____

12. How would you rate your experience in this park?
    1 EXCELLENT   2 GOOD   3 MEDIOCRE   4 DISAPPOINTING

13. How would you rate the park's facilities?
    1 EXCELLENT   2 GOOD   3 MEDIOCRE   4 BAD CONDITION

14. What nature-related did you engage in while in this park?
    1 JUNGLE EXCURSION   2 MOUNTAIN TREKKING   3 BIRD WATCHING
    4 WILDLIFE WATCHING   5 BOTANY   6 FISHING/HUNTING
    7 CAMPING   8 HIKING   9 VISIT INDIGENOUS CULTURES
    10 BOAT TRIPS   11 OTHER (specify _____

15. List up to four things you liked best on your visit to this park (you may consider for instance
    installations, food, guards, information, natural features:
       1 _____   2 _____
       3 _____   4 _____

16. Please list up to four things you did not like:
       1 _____   2 _____
       3 _____   4 _____

17. In your opinion, what should be done to improve the quality of the visit and experience?
    Consider transportation, logistics, guide, technical information (i.e. maps, guide books),
    accomodation, food, etc.?
    _____
    _____
    _____
    _____

18. Do you think this park is or will be facing any particular problems? If yes, specify:
    _____
    _____
    _____
    _____

19. What is the approximate annual income of you and your family?
    1 LESS THAN US$ 5,000
    2 LESS THAN US$ 10,000
    3 OVER US$ 10,000
    4 OVER US$ 20,000
    5 OVER US$ 30,000
    6 OVER US$ 40,000
    7 OVER US$ 50,000
    8 OVER US$ 100,000

(you may tear off this section and keep it)

**ONCE AGAIN, THANK YOU VERY MUCH FOR TAKING THE TIME TO PARTICIPATE IN THIS
QUESTIONNAIRE. IF YOU WANT TO KNOW MORE ABOUT THIS STUDY AND ITS RESULTS
PLEASE FEEL FREE TO WRITE TO THE WORLD WILDLIFE FUND IN WASHINGTON, D.C.,
ATTENTION OF SUSANNE FRUEH, PROJECT DIRECTOR, NATURE TOURISM.**

APPENDIX D

Maps of WWF Protected Area Case Studies

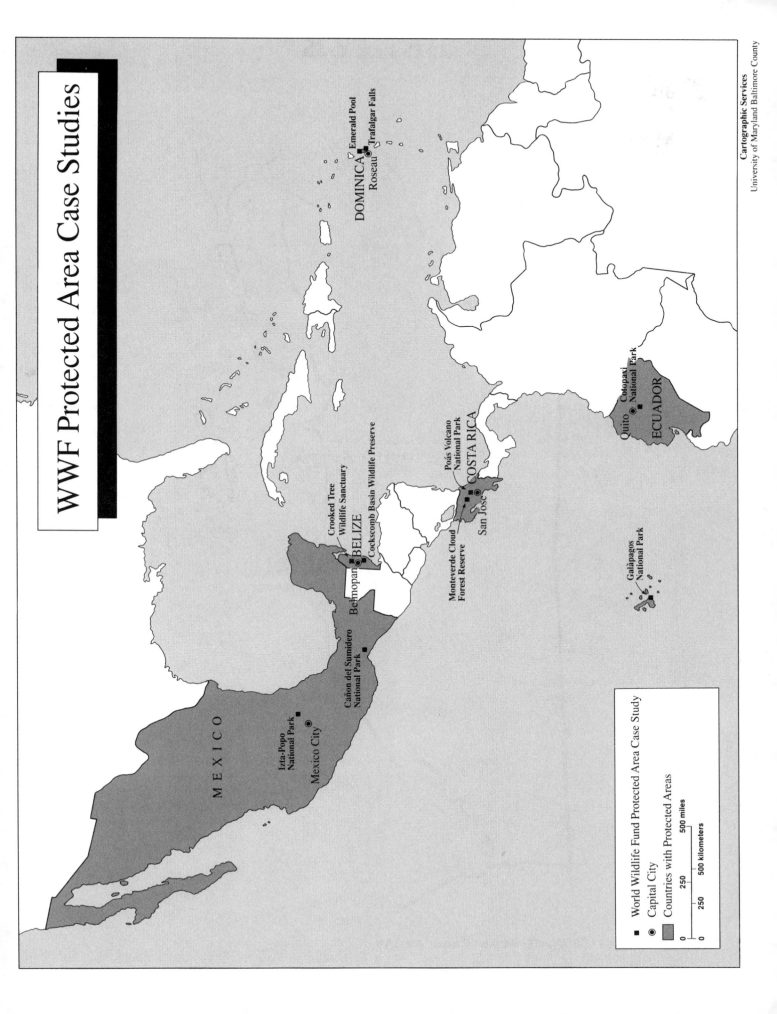

WWF Protected Area Case Studies

MEXICO

Izta-Popo National Park

Mexico City

Cañon del Sumidero National Park

Crooked Tree Wildlife Sanctuary

BELIZE

Cockscomb Basin Wildlife Preserve

Belmopan

Poás Volcano National Park

COSTA RICA

Monteverde Cloud Forest Reserve

San José

DOMINICA

Emerald Pool

Trafalgar Falls

Roseau

ECUADOR

Cotopaxi National Park

Quito

Galàpagos National Park

Legend

■ World Wildlife Fund Protected Area Case Study

◉ Capital City

Countries with Protected Areas

0	250	500 miles	
0	250	500 kilometers	

Cartographic Services
University of Maryland Baltimore County

BELIZE

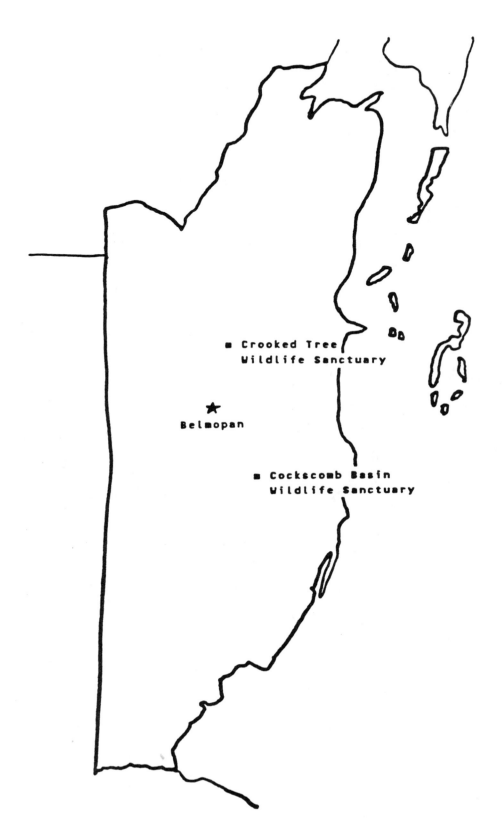

■ Crooked Tree
Wildlife Sanctuary

★
Belmopan

■ Cockscomb Basin
Wildlife Sanctuary

■ WWF Protected Area Case Study

COSTA RICA

■ Monteverde Cloud Forest Reserve

■ Poás Volcano
National Park

★
San Jose

■ WWF Protected Area Case Study

DOMINICA

■ Emerald
   Pool

■ Trafalgar
   Falls

★ Roseau

■ WWF Protected Area Case Study

ECUADOR

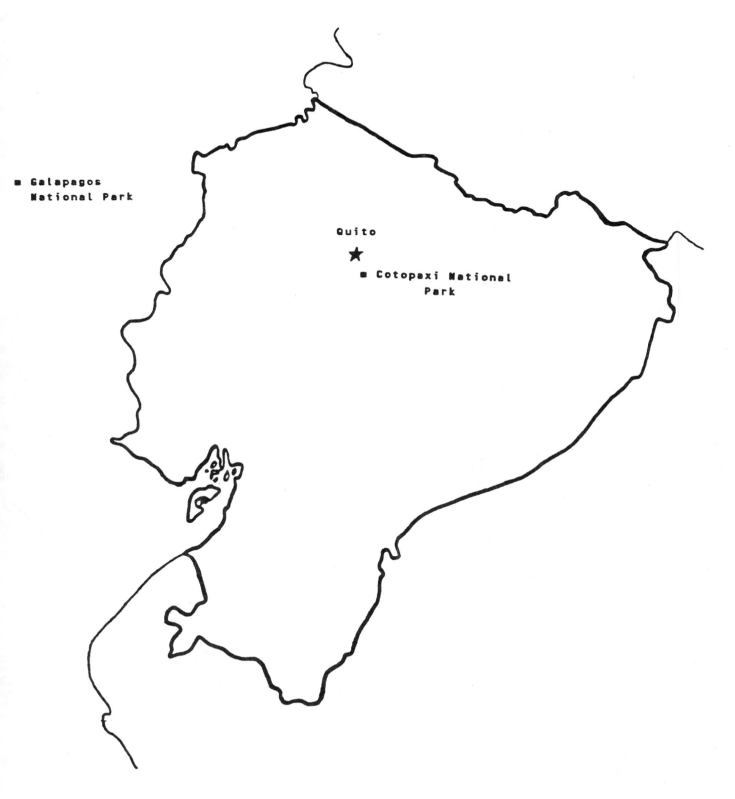

■ Galapagos
  National Park

Quito
★
■ Cotopaxi National
         Park

■ WWF Protected Area Case Study

MEXICO

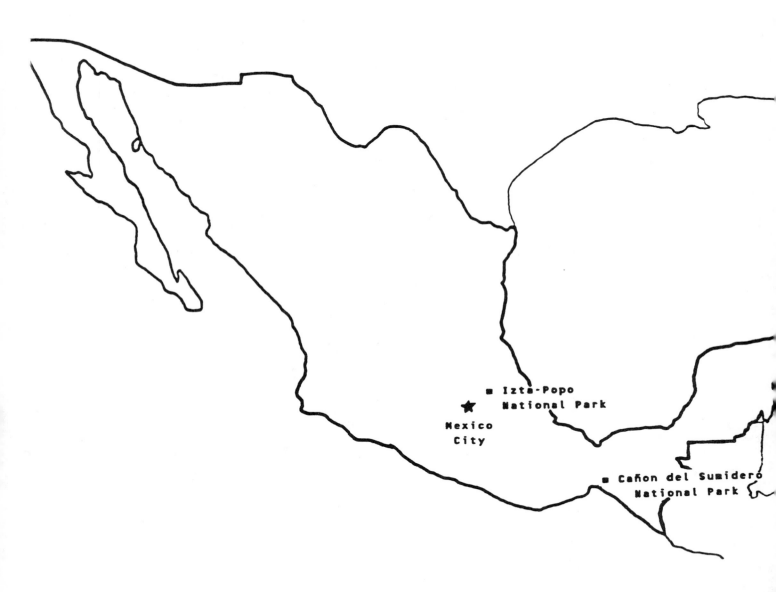

■ Izta-Popo
National Park

★
Mexico
City

■ Cañon del Sumidero
National Park

■ WWF Protected Area Case Study

ABOUT THE AUTHOR

Elizabeth Boo graduated from the University of Notre Dame in 1981 with a B.A. in political science. She then spent a year in Tepatitlan, Mexico, teaching English. In 1986 she completed an M.A. at George Washington University in international affairs, with a concentration in economic development of Latin America. She began working with the Latin America and Caribbean Program of World Wildlife Fund in 1986, where she currently serves as Ecotourism Program Officer.